AN INTRODUCTION TO THE GREEK THEATRE

AN INTRODUCTION
TO THE
GREEK THEATRE

BY

PETER D. ARNOTT, M.A., Ph.D.

WITH A FOREWORD BY
H. D. F. KITTO

MACMILLAN

338962

First edition 1959
Reprinted 1961, 1962, 1965, 1971, 1973, 1977, 1982 (twice), 1985

Published by
THE MACMILLAN PRESS LTD
London and Basingstoke
Companies and representatives
throughout the world

ISBN 0-333-07913-2

Printed in Hong Kong

FOR EVA

FOREWORD

BY

H. D. F. KITTO

THIS is a book that can be warmly commended to those who read Greek plays, whether in the original or in translation. There is no scarcity of books on Greek drama, and books on the Greek theatre are not hard to come by ; but the field was wide open for a book like this, written by one who is equally at home in Classical scholarship and in the actual theatre. It gives the reader of the plays just what he needs, and what he will not easily find elsewhere. Indeed, my one complaint is that it was not available when I myself began reading the plays ; it would have saved me much confusion.

For Greek plays, at first, are not easy. Translation may — at a cost which Mr. Arnott fairly assesses — relieve the reader from the burden of grappling with the Greek language, but the language is by no means the only difficulty. I well remember how Greek drama was first presented to me, by teachers and commentators : everything was so negative. Thus, the Greek dramatist was under the strange restriction, never convincingly explained, of being allowed to use only three actors ; he had no curtain, and therefore could not change either the scene or the time of the action ; tradition dictated to him a stiff form of dialogue, and insisted that he should use a chorus ; further, by tradition he was not allowed to invent his own plots, but had to use myth, so that his audience knew the outline of the story already. It all gave the impression that since there was so much that the Greek dramatist could not do, it was surprising that he did anything at all.

This was the result of starting with our modern theatre in mind. There is a natural inclination to think of our own theatre, and the drama written for it, as the 'natural' form, and of other forms as being deviations from it, or imperfect approximations to it. Mr. Arnott's first chapter firmly draws the distinction between drama based on convention and drama — our own — based on illusion. Doing this, he puts the reader on the right path from the beginning.

In writing this book Mr. Arnott has enjoyed enviable advantages, and has made full use of them. He is a Classical scholar who has had much experience of Greek plays in the theatre, as actor, as producer, as translator. One may suspect too — though he says nothing about it in these pages — that he has learned much from his own interesting and impressive performances of Greek tragedies and comedies with puppets, in a scale-model of the theatre in Athens. Certainly the writer of this Foreword has learned much from them. For example : the Theatre of Dionysus, in the second part of the fifth century, had an architectural background, suitable enough when the action of a play was supposed to take place before a temple or a palace ; but what did the dramatist do when the imaginary scene was open country ? Some writers on the Greek theatre have supposed that somehow the architectural back-scene must have been concealed ; others have been more cautious. One of Mr. Arnott's performances showed me that the problem does not exist. The *Frogs* of Aristophanes begins with a scene in which the architectural background is natural and acceptable ; then the imaginary background becomes the River Styx, and a dismal waste-land beyond it. Watching Mr. Arnott's lively little figures, and listening to their comic lamentations on their desperate fix, one was as indifferent to the architectural background of his small stage as to the fact that one was — just as incongruously, when you come to think of it — sitting in a comfortable chair. The poet's language took complete control ; the total absence of visual illusion stimulated rather than obstructed the spectators' imagination. One was in the Greek theatre, and any attempt to disguise the fact would have been silly. It was a complete demonstration ; the question was answered.

In so far as a book can do it, this one will do for the reader of the plays what he needs : it will take him out of our own time and place, out of our theatrical conventions, and set him down in Athens, in the Theatre of Dionysus, in the Athenian conventions, and in the Greek sunshine. Many readers of the plays, some of them quite experienced readers, will, I am sure, be grateful to him.

PREFACE

EXCELLENT and inexpensive translations are rapidly bringing Greek drama to a wide new public, including many with no previous knowledge of the Classics. At the same time many schools and universities are supplementing or superseding formal instruction in Greek and Latin by courses in classical literature in translation. It is for such a public that this book has been written. It attempts to give, within a small compass, an account of the background of the plays — their origin, composition, setting and audience. Four plays, each representative of a class, have been selected for individual study. A chapter on Roman comedy has also been included, as it is only through Rome that we can appreciate the characteristics of later Greek work.

Two points must be made clear from the start. This is essentially an introduction. It hopes to fill a place midway between the few pages which commonly precede texts and translations and the specialist works which the average student has neither the time nor the interest to read. So this book can only point the way ; it hopes to provide enough to make the theatrical context of the plays intelligible, but anyone desiring more must turn to the hundreds of books on special aspects of this difficult and fascinating subject.

Secondly, it must be stressed that few things about the Greek theatre are certain. As far as the design of the stage buildings is concerned, lack of archaeological evidence for the early period forces us back on inferences from the plays themselves and other writings. So with the early history of the drama. On many points conflicting theories have arisen which may never be reconciled. I have tried to show the most important points of disagreement, but for the most part only claim to give the most probable view. The reader will be safe as long as he remembers that this may not be the correct, and is certainly not the only one.

'*Drama*', the Greek for 'play', means literally 'something done' not 'something read'. Every attempt has been made to present the plays as products of a living theatre, written to please a keenly critical audience, and not as Great Literature.

This has not, unfortunately, been the criterion employed by history. Only some plays survived on their merits ; others were preserved from academic interest or by accident. A great deal has been lost that would be invaluable in reconstructing the theatre of the time. But on the whole we have been lucky. The surviving plays show the Greek Theatre in all its aspects, one of the most fascinating art-forms that has ever existed.

My thanks are due to those who have helped me write this book : to Professor R. E. Wycherley for his consistent encouragement and for countless valuable alterations and corrections ; to Mr. A. D. Fitton-Brown, to whose great knowledge and penetrating criticism I have been indebted throughout ; and to Miss Eva Schenkel, who has saved me from many lapses into obscurity. But most of all I must express my gratitude to the audiences for whom I have produced and performed the five plays selected here for special study — the only way, when all is said and done, to get to know a play. Their reactions and questions have led me to venture on this book, in the hope that it will introduce many more to the wonder of the Greek theatre.

LANCING, SUSSEX
June 1958

ACKNOWLEDGEMENTS

THE author makes grateful acknowledgement to the following for permission to quote copyright material :

Messrs. George Allen & Unwin, Ltd., for the extracts from Dr. Gilbert Murray's translations of Aristophanes' *Frogs* and Euripides' *Electra* and *Rhesus* ; Messrs. G. Bell & Sons, Ltd., for the extracts from B. B. Rogers' translation of Aristophanes' *Birds* ; The Bodley Head, for the extracts from Rex Warner's translations of Aeschylus' *Prometheus Bound* and Euripides' *Medea* ; The Clarendon Press, Oxford, for the extracts from Dr. Gilbert Murray's translation of Aeschylus' *Prometheus Bound*, and from J. E. Powell's translation of Herodotus' *Histories* ; Messrs. Dennis Dobson, Ltd., for the extract from *New Theatres for Old*, by M. Gorelik ; Messrs. Rupert Hart-Davis, Ltd., for the extract from *Around Theatres*, by Sir Max Beerbohm; the Editors of the Loeb Classical Library, for the extracts from A. S. Way's translation of Euripides' *Cyclops* and *Hippolytus* ; Messrs. Methuen & Co., Ltd., for the extract from *Greek Tragedy*, by Professor H. D. F. Kitto ; Messrs. Penguin Books, Ltd., for the extracts from Aubrey de Selincourt's translation of Herodotus' *Histories*, and from E. F. Watling's translation of Sophocles' *Electra*.

CONTENTS

ILLUSTRATIONS

(between pages 48 and 49)

The Theatre of Dionysus in Athens: view from the Auditorium

The Theatre of Epidauros, before reconstruction
(Photograph by John Pollard, Esq.)

The Theatre of Delphi
(Photograph by Philip Lace, Esq.)

Two views of the Theatre of Sicyon, showing layout of stage buildings
(Photographs by John Pollard, Esq.)

The Theatre of Dionysus in Athens: Orchestra with Central Altar Base and Earliest Stone Foundations

The Theatre of Dionysus in Athens: Throne of the High Priest and Auditorium with Gangways

Euripides: *The Bacchanals*, performed at the Arts Theatre, Cambridge
(Photograph by Edward Leigh, Cambridge)

Sophocles: *Oedipus at Colonus*, performed in the Greek Theatre, Bradfield College
(Photograph by Kennet Studios, Reading)

CHAPTER I

CONVENTION VERSUS ILLUSION

THEATRICAL fashions change almost as quickly as fashions in dress. Plays are ephemeral things, dying each night at curtain-fall to be re-created by the actors the following evening, and all connected with them is subject to constant change and experiment. Styles of setting, acting and production vary from year to year, and from generation to generation. What may at first be stimulating and provocative soon becomes commonplace, and eventually outmoded and ludicrous. Consider the changes in the presentation of Shakespeare, even within the short compass of the last sixty years. The great Victorian actor-managers thought in terms of magnificence. No effort was spared to produce spectacular effects. Scenic artists went for their settings to the exact locations Shakespeare had prescribed, and tried to reproduce them in every detail. *The Merchant of Venice* inspired painstaking representations of the Bridge of Sighs and the Doge's Palace. In the early days of the Stratford Memorial Theatre, no production of *As You Like It* was considered complete without a notorious stuffed stag, which stood among the painted trees to lend verisimilitude to the Forest of Arden. The dramatist's words were submerged under gallons of paint and acres of canvas. It was not unusual for the manager who had commissioned these colossal works to appear on the stage at the beginning of a new scene, bowing to the applause which greeted each manifestation of realistic art.

A new generation found these displays cumbersome and unwieldy. They realized that Shakespeare's greatest qualities, the swift current of action and the clear flow of thought, were only impeded by such means. So a reaction took place, and for a brief time the theorists dominated the theatre. Gordon Craig conceived settings which, though towering and impressive, should be 'timeless' and capable of moving with the action. His projects for Shakespearean scenes were not reproductions of any one location, but arrangements of screens roughly suggesting architectural forms, indicating the mood of the scene rather than its background. Craig's theories, though mainly confined to paper, had a decisive effect in liberating the stage from the tyranny of Victorian realism. William Poel sought to restore Shakespeare's speed and freedom by returning to the form of the Elizabethan theatre, a bare, open platform on which the scene was suggested only by the actors' words, with a minimum of properties.

Tastes changed yet again. Audiences began to long once more for colour and excitement, and to crave titillation for the eye as well as for the ear. So the 'twenties brought successive waves of experiment. Each new movement in the world of art had its repercussions in the theatre. We had Cubist Shakespeare, Expressionist Shakespeare, Constructivist Shakespeare, *Macbeth* performed in aluminium screens and a *Lear* lasting five hours. Some of this was inventive and stimulating, but much merely bizarre. Present-day productions favour the formal-decorative school, in which settings, though not realistic, are designed to flatter the eye and contribute a beauty over and above their function in framing the action. Yet there are signs that this phase too is on the wane, and that we shall soon be back on the bare platform of Shakespeare and of Poel, where nothing stands between the audience and the author's words.

As with scenery, so with acting. There is a wide gulf between Irving's sonorous periods and the mannered precision of Gielgud. To modern listeners Irving's distorted vowels, rolling declamation and exaggerated pauses sound ridiculous, and only fit for parody, yet in his own day they were acclaimed as the perfection of acting and Queen Victoria was upset by his 'realism' in performing *The Bells*. Watching old films of Sarah Bernhardt, we see only a grotesque puppet, arms flaying like a windmill ; yet she moved audiences to tears in *La Dame aux camélias*, the very performance which amuses us now. To them she was the divine Sarah, to us only a museum piece.

Only rarely does a company succeed in preserving a style of acting or presentation beyond its normal span of years. The Russian Ballet still employs settings to which Victorian audiences could have taken no exception. The extravagant *décor* for *Romeo and Juliet*, with its tiered arches and disappearing vistas of steps, would have delighted Irving and Beerbohm Tree. The Comédie-Française has kept alive a tradition of classical acting which has come down with little change from the days of Racine and Corneille. In England the D'Oyly Carte Opera still presents its works almost exactly as they were done when Gilbert and Sullivan first wrote them. Every movement, word and gesture is codified and established by rigid tradition, and woe betide the reckless innovator who would dare to alter them. So the Savoy Operas are a living relic of the past, an accurate picture of comic opera production at the turn of the century.

If sixty years can bring about such changes, what transformations have centuries not produced ? Every age and country has introduced its own theatrical conventions. The most exciting thing about the theatre is its constant state of flux, its responsiveness to artistic movements, social changes and scientific developments. It is the mirror of nature in more senses than one. Every new trend finds its echo in some department of the theatre. Much we accept as indispensable, other times and countries would find distracting, and the reverse is equally true. What would we think, for example, of a functionary dressed in green who came on the stage periodically to attend to the lights ? To an eighteenth-century audience this was quite normal. The Elizabethans would have objected to a curtain cutting them off from the stage. The Greeks would have found it abnormal to have to watch a play in a darkened hall. A play lasting only two and a half hours would have been considered by the Victorians a grossly inadequate evening's entertainment.

If stage conditions are so transitory, what is the point in studying them ? It is true that a great play can always transcend the conditions for which it was written. *Hamlet* has been played in a thousand and one different styles — on a simple platform devoid of trappings, and against the candelabra and painted backgrounds of the eighteenth-century playhouse ; against lofty creations of pasteboard castles and settings more reminiscent of a builder's yard ; in the open air before a row of trees, and with all the resources of the modern cinema ; in costumes of all periods from early Scandinavian to modern. It has been cut, altered, added to and rewritten to satisfy every whim of designer and producer, and still remains a great play. Whatever misapplied human ingenuity can do to it, the nucleus remains, to be examined and interpreted afresh by new generations. Though each eccentricity of presentation dies, *Hamlet* lives on. Yet we cannot understand the play fully without some knowledge of the Elizabethan playhouse. A dramatist is a man of the theatre ; this may be a truism, but it is too often ignored. He writes for an audience, to reach which his work must comply with the practical conditions of the theatre of his time. Any author ignoring this primary knowledge — Seneca, say, or Byron — will produce work that is neither one thing nor the other, a treatise in dramatic form.

Although in writing his play a dramatist may be inspired by the highest philosophical conceptions, its ultimate form will be dictated largely by the practical and humdrum, by whatever styles of acting, setting and production are currently in vogue. The construction of a scene may be determined by the interplay of Good and Evil, or by the position of a trap-door. To understand the dramatist's thought, we must know his conception of Good and Evil ; to understand the shape of his play, we must also know about the trap-door. So we study the history of theatrical conditions not from an idle archaeological interest, but to see what advantages and limitations they offered the creative mind, and to what extent the shape of the play depended upon the shape of the play house.

Let us begin by making a distinction. It may seem obvious enough to go without saying, but it must be insisted upon, as it is the basis of the present study. There are, broadly speaking, two sorts of theatre, that of convention and that of illusion. The theatre of convention is like the child who puts a ring of paper on his head, stands on a chair and proclaims 'I'm the king of the castle'. The child who dresses in a detailed copy of a cowboy suit represents the theatre of illusion. Both involve pretence ; the difference lies in the degree to which the pretence is admitted. Each type has come into prominence at different times and in different countries. Sometimes, though rarely, they exist side by side. Our own time is largely dominated by the theatre of illusion.

This presents an imitation of life. It makes only one demand of its audience, that they should imagine themselves invisible spectators of events involving another group of people. 'When the curtain rises', says the playwright, 'you are going to watch an episode in someone else's life. It may be comic or tragic, but it will be presented in the terms in which you yourselves live. The characters will dress like real people, and speak the sort of language that you speak. Our scene-designer has helped by making the settings as lifelike as possible. If the action takes place in a drawing-room, you will see that drawing-room represented. In fact, you will experience the sensation of taking the wall off a house and looking inside. You can see the inhabitants, but they cannot see you.'

So speaks the illusionist playwright. An exact imitation of life is impossible. Life is full of loose ends, and the play must be tidy. Life's problems are confused by all sorts of unexpected irrelevancies, which must be pruned away in the theatre to provide the audience with one clear-cut issue on which to focus its attention. One function of art is to impose order on the chaos of everyday existence. Life goes on without ceasing, but the play must be divided conveniently into acts, to allow the audience to smoke and drink their coffee in the intervals, and end in time for them to catch their last trains home. Each of these punctuations must be accompanied by a heightening of interest, to keep them wondering what will happen next. At the end the problem must be resolved, to send them home satisfied. Life is not so conveniently arranged.

But though the illusionist drama cannot imitate life exactly, it tries hard. Its aim is authenticity of background, dialogue and situation. Perhaps to-day it has reached its logical conclusion in two of its manifestations. The first is the serial drama of family life, well known on radio and television, which takes such pains to ensure accuracy that devotees attribute a real existence to the characters, even sending them letters and presents. The second is the film. Authenticity on the stage can only go so far. Although producers have gone to vast expense and used great ingenuity in portraying horse races, ship-wrecks or eclipses of the sun, such effects are possible only in large and elaborately equipped theatres. Stage realism has always been limited by mechanical difficulties. Scientific progress has reduced them ; thus the superseding of gaslight by electricity made possible the exact reproduction of natural lighting conditions, which could not be attempted before. The camera has removed the last of these limitations. With its aid, and the financial resources of the producing companies, complete authenticity can be obtained. Scenes may be taken in the exact locality in which their author envisaged them. Illusion is complete, and realism has reached its goal.

The predominantly illusionist theatre of our own time may blind us to the fact that any other sort exists. But there have been, and still are, theatres in which the direct imitation of life is the last consideration. Let us imagine ourselves at a performance of the Nō theatre in Japan, which has preserved its style and traditions unchanged for centuries, and still flourishes side by side with the modern theatre influenced by Western standards. There is no curtain, no concealment. The stage is a simple square platform, round three sides of which the audience sit. To one side is a small orchestra, which keeps up a continual accompaniment to the play, much as a pianist used to provide a musical background to the early silent films. From the back of the stage runs a long ramp to ground level. Up this the characters enter, all in the same stately manner, pausing two or three times in their progress. On the rear wall is painted a pine tree. This is the only scenic decoration, and remains the same for every play, whether the action is supposed to be taking place in a cottage, in the fields or on the seashore. Nor are the costumes of the characters any more realistic. They are masked, and the colour of the mask indicates their rôle. A warrior, for example, wears a bright red mask, an old woman a white one. The costumes themselves are rich and elaborate. Even a beggar-woman wears long, flowing robes. Though they bear no relation to any costume worn by such char- acters in real life, their colour and design enable the audience, trained to the convention, to recognize at once what their wearers are supposed to be. Movement and gesture are more akin to ballet than to dramatic acting as we know it. They are non-mimetic — not copied from the gestures of real life, but forming an elaborate code in which the tiniest movement has its own significance. An audience trained to interpret them can follow the emotions which the character portrays.

The play now being performed tells the story of a mother searching for her lost child, though unknown to her the child is dead. She wanders through the country-side — this is represented by a walk around the stage — and comes to a river, where she calls to the ferryman to take her across. The river is not seen, nor is the boat. The woman simply makes the action of stepping into the boat, and she and the ferryman squat down facing each other while he goes through a pantomime of rowing. When the crossing is completed he walks off, leaving the woman alone again. All this is clear to the audience without the aid of elaborate scenic representation.

Consider, too, the English theatre of Shakespeare's day. Again a simple platform stage exposed to the elements and surrounded on three sides by the audience. In the rear wall, a curtained alcove behind which may be concealed large properties, such as thrones, to be revealed and used when required. On either side of the alcove, doors to admit the players ; above it, a balcony. The rear part of the stage is covered by a canopy supported on posts rising from the platform. Such was the simple framework of the stage, but an illimitable variety of scenes could be portrayed within it. The balcony could be used to represent the turrets of a castle, a high wall or the balcony of a house, or even the air wherein spirits could tread. When not needed, it could conveniently be ignored. The Elizabethan eye was not offended by the presence of a very solid balcony in what purported to be a battlefield, but accepted it for the convention that it was. Scenes and places are indicated sufficiently by the words of the characters. Jack Cade has only to say 'I climbed into this garden', and we are in a garden; Duncan, 'This castle hath a pleasant seat', and we are before a castle. Prospero's cave, Desdemona's bedroom, the storm-swept heath in *King Lear* — all these are brought before our eyes by words alone, and not by stage pictures.

The dramatist was not afraid to abandon pretence, step outside the framework of the play and make a direct appeal to the audience. The prologue to *Henry V* tells the spectators in no uncertain terms what was expected of them. Do not expect magnificent representations of battles, says the Chorus; pardon

> The flat unraised spirits that have dared
> On this unworthy scaffold to bring forth
> So great an object : can this cockpit hold
> The vasty fields of France ? or may we cram
> Within this wooden O the very casques
> That did affright the air at Agincourt ?
> O, pardon ! since a crooked figure may
> Attest in little place a million ;
> And let us, ciphers to this great accompt,
> On your imaginary forces work.
> Suppose within the girdle of these walls
> Are now confined two mighty monarchies,
> Whose high upreared and abutting fronts
> The perilous narrow ocean parts asunder :
> Piece out our imperfections with your thoughts ;
> Into a thousand parts divide one man
> And make imaginary puissance ;
> Think, when we talk of horses, that you see them
> Printing their proud hoofs i' the receiving earth ;
> For 'tis your thoughts that now must deck our kings,
> Carry them here and there ; jumping o'er times,
> Turning the accomplishment of many years
> Into an hour-glass.

There could be no more eloquent plea for the use of imagination ; and it is imagination which is the keynote of the conventional theatre.

Each kind of theatre has something to offer, and each its peculiar disadvantages. With the illusionist method the playwright has no difficulty in establishing communication with his audience. They do not have to work for themselves or use their imagination. The play is presented in terms with which they are familiar from their own lives, and makes no demands upon their comprehension. Everything is readily identifiable. This method has great value in the documentary type of play, where interest lies rather in the subject-matter than in its treatment. Plays of prison life, to take only one example, have tremendous impact when the minute-by-minute activities of cell block and exercise yard are portrayed on the stage exactly as they happen. Yet to express a dramatic plot in purely realistic terms takes time. The dramatist is not permitted the short cut of direct appeals or statements to the audience. Sometimes his contrivances become too obvious, and we complain that the plot is artificial — that real characters in those circumstances would never have spoken or behaved as the dramatist makes them. The realistic play *par excellence*, except in the hands of genius, must usually limit itself to slighter themes.

The great advantage of conventional theatre is its freedom. When characters are released from the necessity of imitating life, points can be made faster and more clearly. When the action is not confined between the four walls of one setting, it can become more complex and varied. A gross though popular misconception is that the theatre of convention is so by necessity — that

convention is an apology for illusion, when the mechanics
and techniques necessary for reproducing reality are lacking. Nothing could be further from the truth. An age
which could produce the elaborate masques and processional spectacle which delighted Elizabeth I and James I
would not have been defeated by the problems of scene-
painting. Shakespeare and his fellow-writers did not use
it because they preferred not to ; the dramatic genius of
the period found its natural expression in a stage which
was open, unhampered and unconfined. On the other
hand, this greater freedom makes correspondingly greater
demands on the audience. They are no longer passive
spectators, but an integral part of the drama ; they have
to work, and everything depends on the *rapport* between
them and the players. So this type of play demands a
special type of audience, willing to co-operate with the
dramatist and go half-way to meet him. Such audiences
are not always easy to find.

In our own day the realistic drama predominates,
though, as we have seen, now that realism has reached its
logical culmination in the cinema, the stage may have to
turn to other things. One may still see — but too rarely —
plays which do not rely on imitating life. The modern
English school of poetic drama is not afraid to experiment
and return to the conventional method of other ages. In
Murder in the Cathedral T. S. Eliot uses a chorus to establish
the geographical and emotional setting of the play, and
communicate changes of mood. Towards the end, after
the Archbishop's murder, the four Knights step out of
the action to address the audience directly. Like directors
explaining their policy at a company meeting, they
apologize for the necessity of their action, and try to con-

vince the audience by direct argument that what they
have done is for the best. Similarly the plays of Brecht
use short vivid scenes in the barest of settings, punctuated
with song and appeals to the audience, in a manner much
like the Japanese plays. In such work we may see signs
that the pendulum is about to swing in the other direction,
and that a way is open for a return to greater freedom on
the stage.

In ancient Greece the theatre was one of convention.
In its later stages, changing tastes on the part of the
audience, and a new generation of playwrights grappling
with new problems, imposed on it something of a realistic
pattern ; but for the most part the ancient dramatists
found that they could best treat the lofty moral themes
which formed the staple of tragedy, and the penetrating
inquiry into social and political conditions which was
Greek comedy, by leaving themselves unbound by the
fetters of illusion. The methods they employed may seem
strange to us, but were largely the results of the historical
processes by which the drama arose. What these were we
shall discuss in the next chapter.

It must be emphasized here, and cannot be emphasized
too strongly, that what we know about the Greek theatre,
its settings, acting and production, we know mainly by
deduction. To-day, in an age of constant theatrical
activity, interest in theatrical methods is immense. Every
major production is criticized in the popular press, photographed, analysed and recorded. Books on actors' lives,
theatrical history and archaeology, playwrights and producers, are legion. There was nothing like this in ancient
Greece. The Greeks were keenly interested in plays.
They considered, rightly, that the dramatists were a great

moral force in the state. Plays were read and quoted. Passages from them are used as the basis of philosophical discussions. Pithy sayings and striking sentiments were embedded in the popular language and became almost proverbial in their application. Interest in the practical side of the theatre, however, was negligible. We have few direct statements on the art of production. The *Poetics* of Aristotle, a treatise largely concerned with dramatic composition, dismisses the presentation of the plays in a few cursory paragraphs. Antiquarians of later centuries showed some interest in the mechanics of the theatre, but the wide space of time between their own age and that about which they wrote makes their evidence of doubtful value. Thus in reconstructing a picture of the living Greek theatre we have to rely on tantalizing references in other writers, and on the evidence of the plays themselves. Scholars of each generation tend to be influenced, albeit unconsciously, by theatrical conditions prevailing at their own time. So scholars of the last century reconstructed a Greek theatre with all the elaborate scenic effects they were themselves able to see. It is gradually coming to be realized, however, that the methods of the Greek theatre were peculiarly its own, and that it is possible to discover them by careful and objective study. To appreciate their value and significance we must work, not backwards from our own time, but forwards from the very beginnings of drama in remote antiquity.

CHAPTER II

THE ORIGINS AND STRUCTURE
OF THE PLAYS

ANCIENT GREECE is justly regarded as the birthplace of the drama. It is true that records of some sort of 'passion play' survive from Egypt, but it is doubtful whether these religious festivals were dramatic in any strict sense of the word. In the pre-Hellenic civilization of Crete, too, excavations have uncovered large open arenas which may have been used for representations of some sort, but whether for plays, or exhibitions of animals, such as are depicted on Cretan wall-paintings, or simply for processions, can only be a matter of conjecture. The earliest recorded drama as we know it comes from Greece.

Though we speak of 'Greek drama' as though it were the product of the country as a whole, we possess examples of complete plays from one city only, Athens. Native schools of drama flourished in other parts of Greece and its colonies — the comedies of Epicharmus of Sicily had some influence on later authors — but these are known only from fragments or references in other writers. Although every large city had its theatre, some of great antiquity, little evidence of non-Athenian drama has come down to us. This is something of a mystery. We cannot believe that, in the days of keen rivalry between city-states a rich and powerful city like, say, Corinth, would have consented to use Athenian plays. But if there were Corinthian plays, or Theban, or Argive, history has removed all trace and mention of them. So we are forced to base our appreciation of Greek drama on the work of Athens in the fifth and fourth centuries B.C., the tragedies of Aeschylus, Sophocles and Euripides and the comedies of Aristophanes and Menander. However, 'Greek drama' is a convenient phrase, and there is no reason why we should not continue to use it, just as we speak of 'Latin' when to be accurate we should say 'Roman'. It had two main forms, tragedy and comedy, and a third, satyr play, which may conveniently be left till later.

TRAGEDY

How did tragedy arise? Like so much else about the Greek theatre, this is largely a matter of conjecture. No one answer has been found to satisfy all the scholars. It has been suggested, for example, that the presence of tombs and burial-ritual in so many plays points back to a time when they were acted at royal funerals, telling the story of the king's great deeds in the same way as the Egyptians commemorated the lives of their Pharaohs in paintings on the mummy-case. Brief hints in ancient authorities suggest that tragedy sprang up in several parts of the country simultaneously. Arion, for example, the half-legendary poet famous for his escape from pirates on the dolphin's back, is credited with writing some sort of lyric tragedy. These local variations became welded together in the perfected form as we have it. Without doubt, however, the vital factor in the rise of tragedy was its development from choral songs. This is the view now generally accepted by scholars.

Greece was a land of small communities cut off from each other by the mountains, each with its own presiding god and local deities. To these were added the heroes, great men of the past famous in song and story for their deeds of valour and superhuman adventures. As time passed, the historical authenticity of such stories became lost in frequent repetition and addition. Myths grew up around the characters, gradually assuming a more or less fixed form which became part of the folk-lore of the district, remembered and told with pride by the local inhabitants. The Heracles saga is a typical example. We might call these heroes the saints of the Greek religion, men, not gods, but men whose great and noble deeds had lent them something of divinity. Our own country provides parallels in the Arthurian cycle, or the story of Robin Hood.

Gods and heroes were regarded as having the community under their protection. At various times in the year it was necessary for the people to placate them by sacrifices and celebrations in their honour. These would fall at the times of greatest importance to the farming community, sowing, harvest and the vintage, around which their whole life revolved and in which success or failure meant life or death. It was natural at these festivals to celebrate the gods and heroes in song — to tell of the greatness of a god and how he came to extend his protection to the community, or how a certain hero had saved the land from disaster in time long past.

These songs were delivered by choruses, and their composition became a matter of pride and importance.

So there came into existence a body of poems highly dramatic in content though not in form (like Longfellow's *Hiawatha*), recounting the prowess of the god or hero who was the central figure. They were still merely narrative. The chorus made no attempt to identify themselves with the characters of whom they sang. To transform the dramatic poem into drama it was necessary for one member of the chorus to take it upon himself to speak the words attributed to the god or hero in the poem. In the taking of this vital step, drama was born. Consider the verse :

> The king sits in Dunfermline town
> Drinking the blude-red wine ;
> 'O where will I get a skealy skipper
> To sail this new ship o' mine ?'

Once introduce a second speaker to deliver the two lines attributed to the king, and you move from one art form into another.

Tradition ascribes this innovation to one Thespis, and even gives him a date ; he is said to have performed in Athens about 534 B.C. Whether this is true or not, his name has achieved immortality in theatrical jargon — 'actors' and 'Thespians' are synonymous. The significance of the creation of the first actor cannot be over-estimated. It was now possible not only for the actor but for the chorus also to take parts. The actor could play the god or hero, the chorus worshippers, subjects, soldiers, or whatever the story required. It was now also possible to introduce dialogue between actor and chorus. The chorus, as well as retaining their original function as narrator, could also address the actor in character. This dual function of the chorus, as we shall see, is the distinctive feature of the Greek drama.

There was a similar phenomenon in later history, in the birth of the mediaeval drama of our own country. Like the Greek, it had its origins in religious celebrations, this time in the Mass. As a form of worship this is itself highly dramatic, and the Bible stories embodied in it at particular festivals — the Easter story of the Resurrection, or Christ's birth in the stable at Christmas — lend themselves readily to dramatic treatment. Drama began in England, so far as we know, with the Resurrection story. Some priest had an inspiration : the story could be brought home to the people more vividly if instead of being read by one voice, the words of the angel guarding the tomb and of those searching for Christ's body could be given to different speakers. This done, there were at once the rudiments of a play. A similar treatment was applied to other stories. As time went on, the conception was extended. The speakers began to move about the church, using different areas for different parts of the story as they seemed appropriate. The altar could symbolize Christ's tomb, or the manger, and form a focal point for the simple action. Eventually the plays were taken out of the church altogether into the streets. The whole Bible story from the Creation to the Redemption and beyond was dramatized in short episodes, each played by one group of citizens. Comic and topical elements were added. At first purely traditional, the plays came to be written down and evolved into the great local cycles that we still possess to-day. So from the simple inspiration of one priest who wished to bring the Gospel home to his flock came the drama and a considerable body of dramatic literature. This is what Thespis, if Thespis it was, did for Greece.

Once the initial step of separating actor from chorus had been taken, the rest followed easily. The introduction of a single actor made dramatic action possible, and the addition of a second, ascribed to Aeschylus, increased it. Sophocles added a third, in which he was followed by Aeschylus in his later plays, and, except perhaps for one dubious case, the *Oedipus at Colonus* of Sophocles, this number was never exceeded. Although the number of actors was limited, there was no such limit to the number of parts they could play. The peculiarities of tragic costume, discussed in the next chapter, made it easy for the actor to change rôles with the minimum of delay. This enormously increased the flexibility of the drama. Thus the *Agamemnon* of Aeschylus has six characters, which were apportioned between three actors.

The actor's rôle was at first subordinate to that of the chorus. His function was that of interlocutor. In the *Suppliant Women* of Aeschylus, not, as was once thought, the earliest complete play we have, but certainly modelled on early patterns, there are two actors, but they hardly address each other at all — the story is told by the interchanges between actor and chorus. In time the actor's importance increased. When two were used, it was possible for them to address each other without the chorus intervening. Thus another play by Aeschylus, the *Seven against Thebes*, opens with actor and chorus ; after this the action is carried on in a dialogue between two actors. With three there were even greater possibilities. A pattern was evolved of actor-scenes divided by choruses which explained or commented upon the action. With increased emphasis on the actor, the rôle of the chorus slowly declined. In later tragedy its presence is often an embarrassment, and the action could proceed just as well without it. Eventually it was reduced to a mere *divertissement*, a lyrical interlude between scenes.

The difference in function between actor and chorus was emphasized by the way in which they spoke. Actors' parts were usually written in the iambic trimeter, a line composed of three metrical units × – ◡ –, the first foot being either long or short. This metre was regarded by the ancients as most like the rhythms of everyday speech. Choruses were more complex. The choral odes drew on a wide variety of metres which to some extent reflected the emotions expressed — quick and lively, for example, in passages of excitement. As they sang, the chorus danced or performed some appropriate rhythmical movement. A flute-player accompanied them and gave the beat. Actors could also break into lyric metres at moments of heightened emotion. These passages were actually sung, as in opera, and we possess one fragment of music to accompany the *Orestes* of Euripides. It is still difficult to appreciate how these passages would have sounded in the theatre. Greek music was so different from our own that the fragments cannot be rewritten in modern notation with any certainty. We know, however, that music and the dance were integral parts of the performance, and combined the arts in a way that has hardly been equalled since. Much was done by mime, and there were dances expressing many actions and moods.

With the introduction of the actor, as we have seen, the chorus took on a dual function. It could be both actor and narrator, participant and spectator. Elizabethan dramatists used a single speaker as chorus to supply a linking narrative for their scenes, or to indicate the setting.

Shakespeare uses this device several times — in *Henry V*, *Romeo and Juliet*, and *Pericles, Prince of Tyre*, where the chorus is the poet Gower ; in *Henry IV* where it is an allegorical figure, 'Rumour painted full of tongues', and *The Winter's Tale* where the chorus is spoken by Father Time. The Greek chorus was not merely a *compère*. It has sometimes been described as 'the ideal spectator', but this definition is misleading. More accurately, it stood between the spectator and the action, identifying itself now with one and now with the other. This was invaluable to the dramatist and gave him greater freedom of expression. A modern playwright wishing to draw a moral from a scene must write what indications he can into the scene itself and leave the deductions to the audience. He must not allow his actors to speak out of character. In how many modern problem plays have we been left in doubt as to what the author's intentions were ? The Greeks had no such difficulty. Once a scene had been played, the chorus could step out of the picture to comment on it, and he could put into their mouths the conclusions he wished to draw. Thus we have action and commentary alternately.

'Action' is another word we must beware of using in the modern sense. Greek tragedy had little action in our meaning of the word. Though its themes are often violent and bloodthirsty, it confines itself to narration, discussion and speculation. We are led up to the point where some violent deed is going to take place, given the motives for the deed and the story behind it, but the deed itself takes place off stage. It is usually held that Greek taste forbade the representation of death in view of the audience. but there were practical considerations to be taken into account as well. The actor playing the character who died might be needed for another part later in the play. So the death would have to take place off-stage and a dummy substituted for the body. This happens in the *Ajax* of Sophocles. Ajax commits suicide half-way through the play, and the second half is a discussion over his body. The suicide takes place out of sight, a dummy is brought on for the body, and the actor returns later as a new character. In the *Hippolytus* of Euripides, where the death of Hippolytus falls at the end of the play, the device is unnecessary and the death is enacted in full view of the audience. This also happens in the same author's *Alcestis*. Normally an off-stage death is reported by a herald or messenger. Sometimes the body itself is revealed, to form a tableau round which the ensuing discussion centres. This is not to say that the plays lack excitement — far from it — but terror resides in the unseen far more than in the seen, a fact which every good writer of ghost stories knows and many producers would do well to remember. 'Horror comics' are not horrifying but nauseating, because everything is put before our eyes, there is nothing left to the imagination. The excitement of Greek tragedy lies rather in the cut and thrust of debate, the thrill of anticipation, the gradual realization of inevitable disaster, than in the horror of watching a bloodthirsty spectacle.

Tragedy drew its themes mostly from well-known stories — histories of royal houses, or tales of divine intervention in human affairs, which were well suited to its moral purpose. Some poets invented original plots, but none have come down to us, and it is doubtful whether they were ever popular. Thus the audience went to the

23

theatre knowing from the play's title the outline of what they were to see. The element of surprise was largely eliminated — the playwright could not win easy applause by a trick ending, though Euripides comes close to it in his variations on well-known plots. The measure of the dramatist's skill lay in his treatment of his chosen theme. Although the story was fixed, the characterization, message and language were his own. In choral lyrics his skill or lack of it especially revealed itself. His problems were those of the modern dramatist writing an historical play about Henry VIII or Mary, Queen of Scots. What happened to the character is a matter of history, and he cannot alter that by making Henry a bachelor or Mary execute Elizabeth, but the treatment of these stories is capable of infinite variation, depending on where his sympathies lie. The Greeks were even more limited in their themes, and the wonder of their art is that so many plays, and so different, were made on so few subjects. One merit of this limitation was that the dramatist needed to waste no time in introducing characters or building up to a situation. His audience already knew them, and did not need programme notes, written or spoken, to help them. A later comic poet objects that tragic writers have only to let their characters announce who they are and the audience knows everything, but the comic writer, using original plots, has to start from scratch.

'Tragedy' did not necessarily have for the Greeks the meaning it has for us, of a play with an unhappy ending. True, most Greek tragedies do end unhappily, with the central character involved in some sort of disaster. The protagonist struggles against fate and usually loses. But some of the greatest plays end in reconciliation, for example the cycle of three plays known as the 'Oresteia' trilogy, by Aeschylus; though we have only one play of his Prometheus trilogy, it has been conjectured that at the end the opposing elements are reconciled. His *Suppliant Women*, too, ends tranquilly. Some plays by Euripides would now be called romantic melodramas rather than tragedies. His *Helen* argues that this lady was not taken to Troy, but replaced by a ghostly image created by the gods in her shape to start the Trojan War; Helen herself was all the time in Egypt. The play tells how her husband Menelaus is shipwrecked on the Egyptian coast on his return from Troy; he is in imminent danger from the savage king, but is rescued by his wife's cunning. Together they escape and sail happily away. The Greeks used 'tragedy' rather in the sense of a serious treatment of some moral question as personified in characters of myth or legend.

COMEDY

Any celebration which unites mutual friends and acquaintances tends to fall into the same pattern. In one corner of the room, the amateur politician holds forth on the blunders of the government, announcing in no uncertain terms how he would go about remedying them. In another, two guests indulge in a ridiculous argument which began in some silly proposition by one of them, that is now being defended and attacked with all the inventiveness in their power. In the middle of the room someone else comes in for good-humoured teasing. There is singing and dancing; someone with a talent for that sort of thing may even recite some impromptu verses, not great art but tolerantly received in the joy of the occasion. Set this situation back a few thousand years and you have the beginnings of comedy.

We are in a small Greek village. It is summer, and the grapes have just been gathered in. The vintage has been good and the people are happy. It is a time for celebration and rejoicing. There is drinking and singing. The villagers gather round to watch a dance. In the spirit of festivity normal codes of restraint and good behaviour are relaxed. Things normally frowned upon are tolerated or overlooked. The brighter spirits of the village make the most of their opportunity. They poke fun at authority — the village elders, the warriors, even the gods. The native Greek genius for dramatic expression finds a vent in topical songs, stump speeches and farcical arguments. They entertain each other with comic antics, horseplay and buffoonery, much of which moderns would find grossly obscene, but for the simple villagers was natural and harmless, springing from the circumstances in which they lived — fertility, birth and regeneration were part of their lives and as legitimate for humour as anything else. The humour of the Greeks was the spontaneous self-expression of a fun-loving people.

In such simple amusements we may guess that comedy arose. Its choral origins may be found in the *komos*, a dance or procession by a group of revellers who may have worn animal costumes — an old Attic vase shows men riding on dolphins and ostriches, accompanied by a flute-player. This perhaps embodied a debate and ended with a revel. When comedy acquired literary form it kept many of the elements of these rustic celebrations. As in tragedy, three actors were generally used, with a chorus, but the pattern of comedy was looser and more variable. Within this framework the same forms of humour recur. Many plays contain an *agon*, a farcical debate in which opposing sides argue some nonsensical question with a wealth of irrelevancy and comic illustration. Again, midway in the comedy the chorus usually addresses the audience directly on some topical point which has little or nothing to do with the plot of the play. This address (the *parabasis*) may deal with current politics, social reform, the conduct of the war or anything of current interest. These elements are woven into a pattern of short scenes interrupted or assisted by the chorus according to the poet's whim. The number of characters is far larger than in tragedy — the *Birds* of Aristophanes has twenty-one speaking parts divided among three actors, besides supers and walking-on parts — and the play usually ends in a procession, dance or revel.

Tragedy was already provided with plots, but comedy had to invent its own. They were usually highly topical, satirizing personalities and movements of the day, often bringing in living people by name or thinly disguised. Comic playwrights enjoyed unlimited licence. Similar attacks made from the stage to-day would provoke a barrage of slander actions. Sometimes they overstepped the mark and were punished, but a society as secure as the Athenian democracy at its greatest could permit much that a weaker state could not have tolerated. Even the gods were not immune. There has been no later parallel to the way in which the Greeks permitted their gods to be shamelessly mocked on the stage. The mediaeval mind permitted the leavening of Bible stories with topical, often broad, humour, but even this broadmindedness would not have been equal to the spectacle, say, of the Twelve Apostles engaging in knockabout comedy. Yet this would have been but a mild equivalent of what the Greeks tolerated and frankly enjoyed.

There was humour for all tastes. A favourite device was to parody the high-flown language and stage conventions of tragedy. Subtle wit was followed by slapstick, obscenity by scintillating paradox. In contrast, the choral lyrics were often of real beauty and rank among the most delightful of poetry. Greek comedy remains unique as an art form. No other age has been quite able to equal it. The nearest parallel to-day would be a combination of intimate revue and pantomime. The Gilbert and Sullivan operas, too, have much in common with Greek comedy. Aristophanes' plots are echoed in those of the Savoyards. With the *Frogs*, satirizing the pretentiousness of tragic poets, we may compare *Patience*, which parodies the aesthetic movement of Oscar Wilde and his school ; with *Women in Parliament*, a sardonic picture of female government, *Princess Ida*, whose theme is education for women. The *Wasps* and *Iolanthe* both ridicule the law courts, the *Birds* and *Utopia Limited* the problems of an ideal state. Notorious politicians are attacked in the *Knights* and *H.M.S. Pinafore*. The operas have kept public favour because of the charm of their music, but the danger of topical comedy is its limited appeal. Tragedy, dealing with eternal themes, carries a message for all ages, while comedy, dealing with the personal and topical, is less enduring. We lose the point of many jokes in Greek comedy through knowing nothing about their targets, and to re-create the background of the plays involves more study than the average reader can give. The more topical a play, the less likely it is to endure. Thus we no longer find much humour in Aristophanes' *Knights*, a satire on late fifth-century Athenian politics, and Gilbert's libretto for *Patience* could well be completely rewritten. Aristophanes' *Birds*, however, a more general attack on the problems of empire-building, continues to amuse, and the *Gondoliers* will be funny as long as there are monarchies and republics. A surprising amount of the original spirit of Greek comedy still comes over in productions. Versions are sometimes given with the framework of the original retained and the Greek topicalities replaced by modern.

In the best Greek comedy the chorus was as important as in tragedy, and usually gave its name to the play. As the settings were mostly fantastic, the chorus could be whatever the author's imagination pleased — clouds, birds, storks, cities, wasps. They did not perform the same essential function of standing between the audience and the action. Comedy was not bound by rigid convention, and its greater freedom allowed actors to address direct appeals to the audience as a body or to individuals by name. A frequent source of jokes was for characters to address asides to stage-hands or refer to the workings of the stage machinery, usually conventionally ignored — much as a television comedian raises laughs by commenting on the movement of the camera. These references give valuable information about practical stage conditions.

As with tragedy, the importance of the chorus diminished in time. They were reduced to singing an occasional lyric to enliven the scenes. In the end nothing was specially written for them. Only the note 'Chorus' written at intervals in the play indicates where they were to come in and sing, it mattered not what.

ORGANIZATION

The Greeks had no permanent theatre as we know it. It was impossible for a citizen in search of entertainment to go out any day to see a play. Nor was it a commercial venture, run for profit. Throughout its greatest period it retained the religious significance which was its birthright. Plays were presented not purely as entertainment but as an act of worship, which it was the right and duty of every citizen to attend. Drama became associated with the worship of Dionysus, God of the Vine and the centre of a mystical cult in which his followers found ecstasy and a release from normal inhibitions. His worship came over from Asia Minor, though references to Dionysus stories are also found in pre-Hellenic writings. He became also God of Tragedy, and his image stood in the theatre to watch the plays.

There were three main Athenian festivals, held in the early part of the year — the City Dionysia, Rustic Dionysia and the Lenaea. The first was mainly a tragic, the third a comic, festival. To the City Dionysia people flocked from all parts. It was an occasion of great civic importance, attended not only by the Athenians themselves but by foreigners and visiting ambassadors and delegations. As well as plays, lyric choruses were performed, and various state duties carried out, such as parading the sons of Athenians who had fallen in battle.

The drama was thus an important state responsibility

and financed largely out of public funds. Actors were paid by the state, choruses by private citizens. Anyone wishing to present a play could apply to the city magistrates to be granted a chorus. He was then allotted a *Choregus* — almost 'backer' — a wealthy citizen whose larger income rendered him liable for special duties. It was his task to pay for the training and equipping of the chorus. This was at best an expensive business, though the cost naturally varied with the generosity or meanness of the individual. *Choregi* vied with each other in producing magnificent displays. Festivals were competitive, and a panel of judges awarded a prize to the best group of plays. At the City Dionysia three tragic poets competed, each offering three tragedies and a satyr play, either a cycle on one theme or dealing with different subjects. The normal number of competing comedies was five, reduced to three in war-time. The plays frequently contain appeals to the judges to give their poet the prize. Comedies promise great rewards if they do, and all manner of ridiculous punishments if they refuse. Even tragedy was not above these devices. Three plays of Euripides close with such an appeal.

> O Victory, revered and mighty,
> Rest upon me all my life
> And never cease from crowning me.

The successful *choregus* erected a monument to his victory, and the triumphant poet was a power in the state.

CHAPTER III

THE THEATRE AND ITS EQUIPMENT

I N the structure of its theatre, as in the structure of its
plays, Greek drama remembered its origin. As the
most important element was the chorus, so the most
important part of the theatre, and its distinctive feature,
was the place where the chorus sang and danced. Rain is
rare in Greece, and the people did not need to bother with
covered theatres ; the dancing-place, or *orchestra*, was
simply a large level space cleared at the foot of a rise from
which the maximum number of spectators could have a
good view. Its circular shape was dictated by the lie of
the land, though in the tiny theatre of Thoricos near the
coast of Attica to the south-east of Athens this was
abandoned for an area roughly rectangular, following the
line of the rock. Probably the circular form was ideal,
but varied with local conditions and the time and money
available for construction. In the centre of the orchestra
stood the altar of Dionysus, round which the chorus
danced.

The earliest archaeological remains that we possess, on
the site of the great Theatre of Dionysus at Athens, are
stones marking the rim of such an orchestra, and probably
date from the mid-fifth century. Reconstruction of the
other theatre buildings is difficult. Originally made of
wood, they left no trace ; the stone buildings which

replaced them mostly date from later times when the drama had assumed a different pattern and needed a different sort of theatre. So we have to rely mainly on deductions from the plays themselves, which have produced widely different interpretations. It is the same problem that we have in reconstructing the stage for which Shakespeare wrote, though with no contemporary illustrations or descriptions to help us. Nevertheless it is still possible to trace the development of theatrical architecture in its broad outlines ; the most probable view is as follows.

The actor-chorus division created the need for somewhere where the actors could change their costumes and retire between scenes. Originally this need was filled by a simple hut or tent erected at the edge of the orchestra. The Greek for tent is *skene*, and this, through the Latin *scaena*, gives us our word 'scene'. In time this primitive booth was replaced by a larger and more complicated structure of wood, though still only temporary and removable when not needed, fitted with doors through which the actors could enter. At some time this was decorated with a painted architectural façade, probably in false perspective, though it must be emphasized that this was only decoration and not scene-painting as we know it. Eventually this temporary structure was replaced in turn by a permanent stone building — probably in the last quarter of the fifth century — more elaborately designed to accommodate the new mechanical devices then beginning to be used. It retained the entrance doors — no more than three are needed in any one play — and was decorated with statues of the gods.

In the same period the auditorium was similarly transformed. Originally spectators looked down on to the

orchestra from the bare hillside. Then tiers of wooden
benches were built, later replaced by stone. These ran
more than half way round the orchestra circle ; the space
between either end and the scene building was known as
the *parodos*, and formed the entrance through which the
chorus approached the orchestra. Gangways ran from
the top tier to the bottom, and also from side to side,
allowing the audience to assemble and disperse without
delay. In an auditorium like this a great number of
spectators could have a good view. The theatre at
Epidauros held an audience of 14,000 in ancient times ;
for a festival held there recently, when several ancient
tragedies were revived, these numbers were increased to
20,000.

In reconstructing the fifth-century theatre one point
has aroused more discussion than any other — whether the
actors performed on the same level as the chorus in the
orchestra, or whether a raised stage was built for them in
front of the scene-building. Since the middle of the last
century scholastic opinion has supported the former view.
Against this it may be said that the whole weight of
ancient tradition supports the existence of a raised stage
from the earliest period — though there is, admittedly, no
contemporary evidence ; that several plays demand such
a platform, as we may deduce from the texts ; and that in
no case would the action be impeded by its presence.
Theatres of the fourth and third centuries had stages as
high as ten or eleven feet. Few would attempt to argue
that these were present in the fifth century, but it is reasonable to believe that a lower stage, some four or five feet
high, adjoined the scene-building to give extra height for
the actors above the orchestra, and was connected with

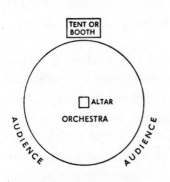

I The simplest elements: dancing-floor and tent for changing.

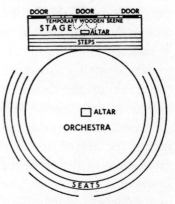

II Beginnings of an architectural form: wooden skene on stone foundations, wooden seats.

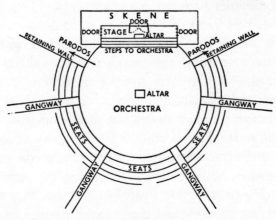

III The theatre in stone.

the orchestra by steps. Absolute proof, as in so many things, is impossible, but in the face of ancient tradition the onus is on those who would argue against it. For the purposes of this book it will be assumed that such a stage did exist, and the reader may accept it or not as he chooses.

The changing pattern of the drama, with its decline in the status of the chorus, brought about corresponding changes in the theatre. When the actors became supreme they were given greater prominence, as we have seen, by raising the height of the stage. Without a chorus the great space of the orchestra was only an embarrassment. It was used for seats, or, under Roman influences, reduced to a semicircle. In the Theatre of Dionysus the orchestra was even made watertight to allow it to be flooded and used for battles between miniature ships. This theatre thus preserves traces of every stage in its development — the first simple orchestra ; stone foundations with slots for posts supporting the wooden scene-building ; the ground-plan of the later stone construction ; and the elaborate, richly sculptured Roman stage.

Although simple in design, the theatre offered a choice of acting areas. The chorus was for the most part confined to the orchestra, where there was room for the compli-cated dances. Sometimes, especially in the early plays where they took a greater part in the action, they moved back against the *skene* and even entered through its doors. The chorus of Furies in the *Eumenides* of Aeschylus came on in this way, appearing in ones and twos instead of up the *parados* in the usual solemn procession, with such devastating effect that the audience was terrified and women gave birth at the sudden shock. At least, so runs the tradition. But the proper home for the chorus was the orchestra ; though they occasionally appeared in other parts of the theatre, they were never there for long.

Similarly, actors used the stage, though there was nothing to prevent them descending the steps to mingle with the chorus or entering up the *parodos*. This was especially useful in processional entrances, which would be long and elaborate. In the *Iphigeneia at Aulis* Clytemnestra and Iphigeneia enter in a chariot ; so does Queen Atossa in the *Persians* and Agamemnon in the play of that name. The funeral processions which the dramatists, especially Euripides, were fond of introducing into their plays could also be displayed to greater effect by bringing them into the orchestra.

A third acting area was the roof of the scene-building. This provided an upper storey which could conveniently represent the heavens, in which gods and goddesses appeared. In one early play by Aeschylus there was an effective tableau of Zeus on high weighing the lives of two warriors in his balance, while on either side of him their divine mothers pleaded for their sons. At the end of the *Medea*, as we shall see, Medea appears above the roof of the *skene* as if in the sky, riding in a snaky chariot. With the same simple symbolism the mediaeval players set God on a higher level in the 'heavens' to look down at the human action taking place below. In the *Prometheus Bound* the whole chorus, representing winged sea-nymphs, made their first entrance on this upper storey, afterwards descending to their usual place in the orchestra. Steps led down inside the scene-building to the ground level. The scene-building could also be used as a dressing-room, for storing the simple properties required by the plays, and to hide the operation of the mechanical devices that the dramatists used to such effect.

There is no evidence that any form of painted scenery,

THE THREE ACTING LEVELS,
SHOWING EKKYKLEMA
IN POSITION

apart from a permanent architectural façade, was used in classical times. In fact the freedom so essential to the plays made such a thing out of the question. Most tragedies are set before a temple or palace, and most comedies before houses or in a street. Thus the simple architectural façade would provide all the background that was required.

It could be identified as the temple of some particular deity by the presence on stage of the appropriate statue, but it is usually enough for the actor or chorus to indicate the scene with a few introductory words : 'Here I sit at the altar of Zeus the Saviour' ; 'Demeter, guardian of this land of Eleusis' ; 'Hail, ancient land of Argos, streams of Inachos' ; 'Twelve weary months have I lain watching by the House of Atreus'.

Much has been written about the so-called Dramatic Unities — unity of place, time and action — of the Greeks, though many when pressed for a definition could only go as far as Dickens's Mr. Curdle : 'The unities, sir, are a completeness — a kind of a universal dovetailedness with regard to place and time — a sort of a general one-ness, if I may be allowed to use so strong an expression'. They were listed as useful rules for the guidance of dramatists by Aristotle. He believed that power lay in economy, and that a play lost force if the action shifted from one locality to another. These precepts were avidly seized upon by later ages. In the classical French drama they are applied in their strictest form. The action never moves outside one setting, and plays no tricks with time. Whatever these Unities meant to the Greeks, they were by no means hard-and-fast rules. Some of the greatest tragedies observe them — the *Oedipus Rex* of Sophocles is played throughout before the palace of Oedipus at Thebes — but many others do not. When we come to consider the *Agamemnon* we shall see that Aeschylus was free to compress the passing of days into a few minutes. His settings were equally fluid. In his *Persians* the action begins in an unspecified place in the Persian capital, and later moves to the tomb of Darius. His *Women of Etna* is set in five different localities. In his *Choephoroi* (*Libation Bearers*) we are first at Agamemnon's tomb, then before the royal palace. In his *Eumenides* the characters travel from Apollo's shrine at Delphi to Athena's temple at Athens. In the latter play the change is more strongly marked by making the chorus leave the orchestra. This was rarely done. It happens again in the *Ajax* of Sophocles, which opens before the tent of Ajax ; he eventually goes off to a lonely spot on the sea-shore, and the chorus is dispatched to find him. When they re-enter we must assume that the scene has changed. In the *Suppliant Women* of Euripides the action begins at Eleusis and ends at Athens, but the location is so confused that at some moments we are not sure where we are. Comedy was even more fluid. The setting changes with unlimited freedom. At one moment we may be on earth, at the next in heaven, and then back to earth again. Action moves from town to country with only the briefest indication. A play with more changes of scene than any other is the *Frogs* of Aristophanes, whose characters travel from the house of the demi-god Heracles across the River Styx in Charon's boat to the gates of the Underworld. Each stage in the journey is well marked, and clearly indicated by the dialogue. Other plays must be imagined as taking place in open country. The *Prometheus Bound* is set on a lonely mountain in the Caucasus, the *Philoctetes* of Sophocles under the cliff-face of a deserted island, the *Cyclops* of Euripides before a sea-cave in Sicily. Again remembering the Elizabethan theatre, we must not imagine that the permanent architectural background was any hindrance. Serving as a house when needed, it could be ignored at will, and the play set wherever the dramatist chose to indicate by the speeches of his character. These contain a wealth of imagery and detail that makes painted scenery superfluous.

Few properties were needed. Apart from the statues of the gods already mentioned, the most important feature of many plays is an altar around which characters sit in supplication, or to which they fly for protection. This was probably not the central altar in the orchestra, which was the cult-altar of Dionysus and associated with the religious side of the festival. It would have been sacrilegious to use it for the plays. There is a story of how Aeschylus, accused of impiety in one of his plays, fled to this altar to escape persecution by the audience. One ancient authority states that the stage 'property' altar was a permanent fixture before the central doors of the *skene*. It appears in so many plays that this may well be true. Some plays require a tomb. In the *Persians* the chorus gather round the tomb of Darius to invoke the dead king to rise again and advise them. In the *Choephoroi* Orestes and Electra invoke their dead father's aid over his tomb. These tombs could also have been represented by the stage altar, particularly since after being used in one scene they are ignored for the rest of the play. This suggests that there was no special scenic structure, as the taut composition of tragedy allowed no time for scene changing during the action.

Of the smaller portable properties, a set of chairs, a throne, a couch, a funeral bier satisfy the simple requirements of the plays. In comedy, where they are used more frequently, they are carried on by the characters themselves and removed in the course of the action to leave the stage uncluttered for the next scene. Sometimes the stage-hands are called out in full view of the audience to assist. Comedy could permit itself such extra-dramatic devices. It is always funny to be taken suddenly 'behind the scenes'.

Though its staging and settings were simple, the Greek theatre used some mechanical devices strange to a modern audience. We have seen the difficulties of representing death on the stage. In some cases the discovery of the body was essential to the plot, as in the *Ajax* of Sophocles, where the dead warrior's companions debate over his body who shall inherit his armour. In such cases dramatic expediency and practical considerations were reconciled by reporting the death through a messenger and then revealing the body on a platform pushed out through the *skene* doors. This platform was known as the *ekkyklema,* 'something rolled out'. Exactly how it worked is unknown. Some think it was a small revolving stage, but the simplest and most practical method, which the author has seen used successfully in modern revivals, is to use a light platform running on rails from inside the *skene* to the front of the stage. When not in use it is lifted out of the way to give actors free use of the door. Some writers who see convention only as an apology for illusion suggest that, as the Greek theatre was incapable of portraying interiors, the purpose of the *ekkyklema* was to show what had been going on inside the house by bringing the interior out before the eyes of the audience. This is misleading. Notions of 'inside' and 'outside' are lost when the *ekkyklema* is used, and to insist on them leads only to confusion. The *ekkyklema* was simply a conventional means of introducing an effective tableau, a function performed in the modern theatre by lighting effects or curtains. Fifth-century dramatists use it frequently, and it is burlesqued in comedies. In the *Acharnians* of Aristophanes the hero calls on Euripides to borrow a tragic costume. Euripides is too busy writing to come down, and so has himself rolled out *in situ* on the *ekkyklema* !

Another favourite mechanical device was the *mechane*, a large crane which lowered characters from above to indicate that they came from heaven, or were flying. Pegasus, the winged horse, was represented in this way, and gods and goddesses appeared in chariots from the skies. It was a common criticism that when a tragic plot became too complicated all the dramatist had to do was introduce a 'god from the machine' (the Latin phrase, *deus ex machina* has become part of our language) to unravel it. In the plays we possess it is not overworked, though inferior playwrights may have used it more often. When the crane was first used is not clear. Its use has been suggested in some cases in early tragedy, but these are doubtful ; it was more probably not employed until the rebuilding of the theatre in stone gave a firm support for its weight. Like other theatrical conventions, it provided material for the comedians to exercise their wit. One character appears flying to heaven on a monstrous dung-beetle, parodying the flying horse, and another appeals frantically to the stage-hand working the crane to let him down when he hears the right cue.

Artificial lighting was both unnecessary and impossible. Torches were frequently introduced for spectacular and processional effects, and the Furies traditionally carried them. In comedy and later tragedy the presence of a lamp on the stage, as in the Elizabethan theatre, indicated night. This realistic touch was a late addition ; in earlier plays the character's words alone established the time of day, just as they did the settings. So with natural phenomena. In two of Euripides' plays, the *Bacchantes* and *Madness of Heracles*, the plot demands an earthquake which destroys the house, and the *Prometheus Bound* ends with Prometheus and the chorus swept down to Hades in a storm. To present such effects realistically would require the combined resources of Bayreuth and Drury Lane. Though Greek ingenuity could have solved the problem, the simplicity of other effects forbids us to think that it was called upon to do so. Such elaborate spectacle would have been alien to every tradition of the Greek theatre. In the 'earthquake' plays the effect is conveyed by the speeches of the characters and choral songs. The chorus of Bacchantes describe vividly what is happening to the palace — the noise of the earthquake, the stonework crumbling, fire blazing from a near-by tomb. This is enough. Once the earthquake has achieved its dramatic purpose, it can be ignored. Characters entering subsequently do not comment on the fact that the house lies in ruins. This lack of observation would be incongruous if the effects of the earthquake had been shown realistically. We should remember the way in which Shakespeare, without the doubtful benefit of elaborate effects, gives the impression of storm at the beginning of *The Tempest*.

MASTER. Boatswain !

BOATSWAIN. Here, master ! What cheer !

MAST. Good, speak to the mariners ; fall t' it, yarely, or we run ourselves aground : bestir, bestir.

BOATS. Heigh, my hearts ! Cheerly, cheerly, my hearts ! Yare, yare ! Take in the top-sail. Tend to the master's whistle. Blow, till thou burst thy wind, if room enough !

and at the end of the scene :

> *A confused noise within;* 'Mercy on us !' 'We split, we split !' 'Farewell, my wife and children !' 'Farewell brother !' 'We split, we split, we split !'

The Elizabethan stage-manager could produce convincing thunder and lightning, but in this scene the picture of a shipwreck is conveyed in words alone. Compare the earthquake scene in the *Bacchantes*.

> DIONYSUS (*inside the palace*). Spirit of Earthquake, rock, rock the
> floor of the earth !
>
> CHORUS I.   Soon the palace of Pentheus
>   Will be shaken to its fall.
>   Dionysus is over the house :
>   Bow down before him !
>
> CHORUS II.   We bow before him.
>   See the stone lintels
>   Crowning the pillars
>   Reeling and shaking
>   Bromios' war cry rings from within.
>
> DION. Kindle the flaming torch of the lightning ;
>   Burn, burn down the palace of Pentheus.

Compare also the language in which Aeschylus paints the great storm at the end of *Prometheus Bound*.

> See, word is replaced by deed ;
> Earth shudders from the shock ; the peals
> Of thunder roll from the depths, and lightning
> Flickers afire ; the whirlwind tosses
> Dust heavenwards, with the four winds dancing
> A giddy reel, challenging each other
> To fight ; sea and sky are as one.

This is not the language of the realistic drama. When the doomed Prometheus embarks on this speech, the audience knows that the storm has come ; they need no other indication.

The Greek theatre was a theatre of the imagination. Simplicity of staging gave full value to the arguments and the beauty of the verse. Great artists prove themselves under limitations, and the Greek dramatists, by limiting themselves so severely in one direction, could give full rein to their abilities in another. The simplicity of the Greek theatre is not that of incompetence but of artistic restraint. Later generations brought a new type of audience incapable of appreciating the subtleties that had delighted their predecessors. They demanded satisfaction for the eye and not for the mind. So tragedy became ornate, spectacle came into its own, and, inevitably, the standard of writing was debased. Even revivals of old tragedies were tricked out with processions and elaborate show to keep the audience entertained. But in its greatest days the keynote of the drama was economy of effect. When two lines in a speech could set the scene, there was no need for anything more.

ACTORS AND ACTING

One aspect of the Greek theatre alone had no room for subtlety, the art of the actor. His effects had to be broad to carry to the limits of the vast audience. With speaking there was no difficulty. Acoustics were, on the whole, excellent. The bowl-shaped structure of the theatre carried the words to the upper tiers of spectators, and the *skene* at the back acted as a sounding-board. In the Theatre of Epidauros, whose design still baffles analysis, every word spoken in the orchestra can be heard clearly at the top, and the sound of a coin being dropped on the stone floor is audible throughout the auditorium. Epi-dauros, with the possible exception of Syracuse, was the first theatre to be designed by a professional architect, and others do not reach the same high standard, but even now, when the scene-buildings are demolished, there is no difficulty in hearing. A Roman writer on architecture, Vitruvius, describes a primitive amplification system for use in theatres. In niches at scientifically determined points in the auditorium were placed jars of different sizes, designed to reverberate to various pitches of the human voice. There is no evidence that this ingenious device was ever used in classical times, and there was certainly no need of it. In Athens to-day opera is still performed in the ancient Theatre of Herodes Atticus, which, though of Roman design, has the same basic principles, and the acoustics are perfect ; every word, every note, is audible throughout the auditorium and beyond.

So much for audibility. Visibility was not so easy. Unlike Victorian children, the Greek actor could be heard and not seen. Confronted with problems quite unlike those facing actors to-day, the peculiar nature of the theatre forced him to develop a special acting technique. Modern acting has been developed for smaller audiences, and the actor relies on this intimacy for his effects. Emotion is expressed by a nod, a smile, a frown ; the inclination of the head, the clenching of the hands, the manner of walking are all important in portraying character. Modern acting is largely naturalistic. Gestures, though exaggerated to carry across the footlights, derive from those of real life.

Such gestures would have been lost in the Greek

theatre. The actor was dwarfed by his surroundings. From the front row he appeared only about four inches high, from the back hardly an inch. Tiny movements would have been invisible to most of his audience. Actions had to be large and sweeping to get across. To some extent this was dictated by the actor's costume. In both tragedy and comedy actors were masked. These masks were partly derived from the drama's religious origins, and partly a conscious device on the part of the first actors. Thespis is said to have experimented with painting his face. As facial expression would have been lost beyond the first few rows, there was no disadvantage in concealing the actors' faces and much to be gained. Women's parts, as in the Elizabethan theatre, were played by men, and masks lessened the incongruity. They were broadly and simply designed to be visible a long way off. The principal traits of the character portrayed could be expressed in the mask, and a simple convention soon arose whereby types of characters had their own types of masks — the tragic hero and heroine, the old men, the messenger were easily identifiable on first appearance. Masks also increased the actors' height by means of a wig-like erection, the *onkos*, on top of the head. In later periods tragic masks lost their earlier simplicity and became merely horrific.

Comic masks were naturally more varied and grotesque. The hard-worked mask-maker, an important theatrical figure, was called upon to represent all sorts of characters, both human and animal. Sometimes he jibbed ; when asked to make a mask of the powerful politician Cleon who was to be pilloried in a play, he refused for fear of the consequences. Comic masks are gross caricatures with

THE THEATRE OF DIONYSUS IN ATHENS : VIEW FROM THE AUDITORIUM

THE THEATRE OF EPIDAUROS, BEFORE RECONSTRUCTION

THE THEATRE OF DELPHI

TWO VIEWS OF THE THEATRE OF SICYON,
SHOWING LAYOUT OF STAGE BUILDINGS

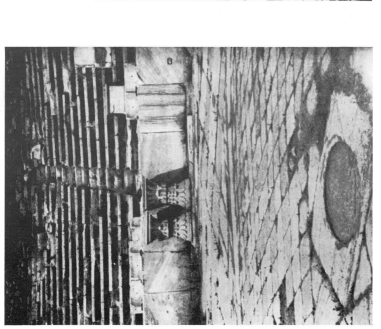

THE THEATRE OF DIONYSUS IN ATHENS

(*Left*) Orchestra with central altar base

(*Right*) Earliest stone foundations, showing slots for wooden posts

THE THEATRE OF DIONYSUS IN ATHENS

(Left) Throne of the high priest   (Right) Auditorium with gangways

EURIPIDES : 'THE BACCHANALS', PERFORMED AT THE
ARTS THEATRE, CAMBRIDGE

(*Above*) Cadmus and Agave with the head of Pentheus
(*Below*) Chorus

SOPHOCLES : 'OEDIPUS AT COLONUS', PERFORMED IN THE GREEK THEATRE, BRADFIELD COLLEGE

staring eyes, bulbous noses and huge gaping mouths.
They were fitted with real hair ; characters are shaved on
the stage, or cut off locks of their hair in tragedy. When
comedy lost its freedom and social significance, and became
a harmless comedy of manners, the masks, as in tragedy,
fell into easily recognizable types — angry old men,
foolish old men, young lover, courtesan, servant, parasite
— and became more realistic.

Tragic actors wore long flowing robes of rich designs
and bright colours which stood out well on the stage and
gave them a statuesque appearance. The costumes are
said to have been copied for the priests' robes at Eleusis.
This gives a good idea of their character — they were
formal vestments, not realistic costumes. On their feet
were buskins (*cothurnoi*), a special boot which came to be
representative of tragedy. It was loose-fitting with a
a thicker sole than usual and fastened high up the leg.
More realistic costumes came later when beggars, for
example, were introduced in rags, a practice attacked for
lowering the dignity of the stage. Generally speaking, the
keynote was richness and magnificence. Sufficient indications of character were given by simple hand properties.
The king carried a sceptre, the warrior a sword. Travellers wore a broad-brimmed hat, heralds a wreath. Furies
traditionally carried lighted torches and the gods their
emblems — Zeus his thunderbolt, Artemis her bow,
Poseidon his trident. Death in the *Alcestis* of Euripides
has black wings. Thus characters could often be recognized by their appearance alone. Heracles with his lion-
skin and club was a familiar figure in both tragedy and
comedy. In other cases the character either announces
himself on arrival or is addressed by name as soon as he

appears. The audience is never left in ignorance for long. The tragic costume, rich, ornate and, later, highly padded, gave the actor a superhuman, depersonalized appearance which suited the rôles he had to play. It added valuable inches to his height and dignity to his movements — it was impossible to make finicky gestures in such costume. The actor changed his character with his mask, which could be done quickly ; it was thus possible for one actor to take several parts without delay or loss of dramatic continuity.

Comic costume was adapted to the freer movements needed for slapstick and burlesque — a short tunic and flat slippers. It was highly padded to give the actor a grotesque, often indecent, appearance. Tragic costume, like tragic language, was often ridiculed on the comic stage. In the *Frogs* Dionysus, God of Tragedy, appears in an attempted disguise, wearing the lion-skin of Heracles over his tragic robe and buskins. The comic actor was highly versatile and had to be something of a quick-change artist. Cast-lists of comedy were long, and he might be called upon to play many short parts in one play with only the briefest intervals for changing costume. As in every age, there were favourite passages of comic by-play which could be inserted anywhere to raise a laugh. One was to singe another character with a lighted torch, the Greek equivalent of the silent film's custard pie. The favourite trick of one comic actor was to belabour his fellow players with his staff.

We know the names of many actors, but in most cases little more. They were as highly trained as athletes — some of them were — and forbidden any form of indulgence before their strenuous performances. Some had

their specialities : Theodorus preferred women's rôles;
Satyrus excelled as a comic slave ; Nicostratus played
messengers. Theatrical traditions ran in families. Carcinus
the tragedian had four sons, one a poet himself and the
others tragic dancers. One of Euripides' sons was an
actor, another a producer, the third went into trade.
Their social status was high — actors were not so vener-
ated again until Irving was knighted — and they were
frequently employed on important diplomatic missions.
There are many stories of professional conceit and jeal-
ousies. Mynniscus, who acted for Aeschylus, criticized
his younger contemporary Callippides for his vulgarity
in women's rôles. Theodorus insisted on being the first
character to speak, as this attracted greater attention to
himself. Another actor refused to go on as a king unless
he had a large enough retinue.

In both comedy and tragedy the link between actor
and chorus was the *coryphaios*, or chorus leader, who
could speak for the whole chorus in conversations with
actors on the stage. Apart from this, the chorus usually
spoke in unison, though sometimes taking individual
lines in turn. The chorus was commonly arranged in
three lines. Weaker performers were kept in the middle,
where they would be less obvious. Thus 'middle row of
the chorus' had the derogatory sense which 'back row'
had in our musical comedies.

Extras and supers were employed to play servants,
soldiers, attendants and the like. Tragic kings and queens
normally enter with an escort. Musicians were also
included in the casts. Flutes, drums, cymbals and trumpets
were used where required. In comedy the flute-players
are sometimes brought on to the stage to take part in the

dance or revel which closed the play. Comedy requires animals of the 'pantomime horse' variety — the *Wasps* of Aristophanes has a comic donkey which must have been played by two men in a skin, and two comic dogs appear in the same play. These men were no doubt specialists who could be called upon when asked.

In the modern theatre responsibility for the finished production is divided between two people, the author who provides the script and the producer who translates it into stage action. The two are rarely combined. Each demands its own training and special skills. In the Greek theatre the poet was originally responsible for everything. He was author, producer and choreographer, even his own chief actor. In time, these duties became too much for one man to manage, and the poet confined himself to writing, delegating the other tasks to specialists. His rôle as actor was the first to be abandoned, partly because some poets were incapable of giving an adequate performance (Sophocles had too weak a voice) and partly because the introduction of prizes for actors, at the City Dionysia in 449, surrendered acting to professionals, who were paid by the state and at first assigned to playwrights by lot, though the obvious unfairness of this arrangement led later to their being given a free choice. So parts came to be written with specific actors in mind, and many of them were famous for their interpretations of one or two rôles. By the end of the fifth century the dramatist had largely withdrawn from stage production, which with the increasing demands of the audience for realism and spectacle had become a highly complicated business. Aristophanes was content to leave several of his plays in the hands of others ; he remarks in one chorus that stage production is a tricky business, which must be learnt from the bottom up — a 'show business' sentiment surprisingly modern in its appeal.

The producer was assisted by a small stage staff. Much of the performance's success depended on the mask-maker and costumier, themselves limited by the sum the *choregus* thought fit to spend. Other assistants worked the machinery, the *mechane* and *ekkyklema*. There was no scene-shifting in the modern sense. One functionary the Greek theatre seems to have dispensed with entirely is the prompter. This gentleman, always present in the modern theatre, is never mentioned in Greek sources until long after the classical period, and comedy contains none of the references we might expect to a prompter who slept on duty or wandered from his post.

When we come to consider individual plays and playwrights we shall see how stage production changed during the fifth century. That there was a change, and a considerable one, is not surprising. The theatre is never static. Changing political and social conditions and new standards of public taste altered the Greek theatre as radically as scientific inventions have our own. At the beginning of the fifth century it was a writers', at the end an actors', theatre. The secularization of the theatre was beginning. It was only a short step to the formation of Actors' Guilds and a new professionalism, with touring companies performing on fit-up stages all over Greece and Southern Italy.

The foregoing chapter has attempted to give some idea of the practical organization of the Greek theatre and the conditions in which the plays were presented. It has inevitably been a brief and summary account. Many of the views advanced rest upon delicate points of scholarship into which it would be tedious for the general reader to inquire. It is hoped, however, that two salient points have emerged. First, the theatre enjoyed the absolute security of state backing and religious protection. Expenses were borne by the state and private citizens in rotation. Dramatists were men of means writing for love of their art and not to earn a living. As in Greek sport, the honour of winning was enough. So, sure of an audience, the theatre never had to play down to its public for commercial reasons or recognize any standards other than moral or aesthetic. Performances were sufficiently rare to prevent the public from growing blasé or indifferent. Plays were not only seen but published, and reached a select reading public where they were discussed and quoted. These are conditions the modern theatre might envy.

Secondly, dramatists and producers counted it more important to stimulate the imagination than to delight the eye, at least for many years. Although actors and chorus were richly dressed, and the great sweep of the theatre provided a noble setting, the audience's imagination set the play. It was words that were important — noble speeches, powerful scenes, beautiful choruses unequalled in the theatre for centuries to come.

CHAPTER IV

THE AUDIENCE

W E have still to consider a group of people who give the drama its meaning, and without whom poet, producer and actors would be useless — the audience. Ancient literature gives many fascinating snippets of information about them, and anyone who has sat among a modern Greek audience will realize how little they have altered over the centuries. The Greeks of to-day go to the theatre with an enthusiasm and lack of reserve that the English keep for football matches. Far less theatrically sophisticated than their Western counterparts, they create an atmosphere of intense excitement, of willing response, which makes the performance a living thing and not a dull repetition. Emotions lie near the surface in Mediterranean countries, and the audience is not afraid to show when it is touched or amused. Sudden turns of plot are greeted with excited gasps ; fine speeches and bravura pieces of acting arouse bursts of applause. The theatre is never ashamed to be theatrical. In the intervals the merits of the play, acting and setting are keenly discussed in a spirit of high critical appreciation. The author has had the enjoyable experience of seeing *Hamlet* played in translation in the open-air theatre of the National Park in Athens. The performance began at ten o'clock at night, and went on until one in the morning ; it was the third given that day, and the demands on the actors' stamina must have been enormous, but who could be jaded before such an audience ? Though the play was as familiar to many of them as it is to us, they followed every twist of the plot as if it were the latest thing out, sighing over Hamlet's repudiation of Ophelia and applauding fiercely the deaths of the last act. Shakespeare would have been at home with such an audience, and many a modern playwright might envy it.

The fifth-century audiences had all these characteristics. Many were well-read and knowledgeable. The fact that the comic poets were able to offer detailed parodies of tragedies years after their original performance and be sure that their audience would appreciate the finer points shows that between festivals the plays were widely read and discussed. Short quotations and allusions were readily identified as well as lengthy parodies. Some might have been deaf to the philosophical implications of tragedy — Aristophanes recognizes this when humorously advocating wings for men in his *Birds*.

> There's nothing like wings to get fun out of things ; when
>   you're bored with a play long and tragic
> You can fly from your seat to get something to eat and be
>   back in the benches like magic.

But everyone would have thrilled to the patriotic fervour of the great choruses in praise of Athens which the tragic poets were not afraid to introduce into their works, such as the following from Euripides' *Medea*.

> Happy of old were the sons of Erechtheus,
> Sprung from the blessed gods, and dwelling
> In Athens' holy and untroubled land.
> Their food is glorious wisdom, they walk
> With springing step in the crystal air.

Here, so they say, golden Harmony first
Saw the light, the child of the Muses nine.

And here, so they say, Aphrodite drank
Of Cephisus' fair flowing stream, and breathed
Sweet breezes over the land, with garlands
Of scented roses entwined in her hair,
And gave Love a seat on the throne of Wisdom
To work all manner of arts together.

Or they could be moved by the spectacle of their own
bravery in the *Persians*, which celebrated the Greek defeat
of the Persian fleet at Salamis and the ignominious with-
drawal of the invaders from their country. There was
something in tragedy for all. In comedy, as we have seen,
there was humour at all levels, satire for the sophisticated
and slapstick for those of simple tastes. There was also
the excitement of recognizing personal targets of the
poet's wit among the audience. Socrates, when being
mercilessly burlesqued in the *Clouds,* is said to have stood
up in his seat for the audience to have a good look at him
and see how poor the resemblance was.

If they found much to approve, the Athenian audience
was never slow to show its disapproval. Unpopular
sentiments spoken from the stage would provoke boos
and catcalls, drumming of feet against the seats and even,
sometimes, showers of stones. It was dangerous to be an
actor in a controversial play. Some of the audience's
strictures seem hard to us. The tragic poet Phrynichus
produced a play about the capture of Miletus by the
Persians in 494. A Greek colony in Asia Minor, this city
had led a revolt against its Persian overlords, and when
defeated was cruelly punished. Phrynichus so moved the
audience that he was fined by the authorities 'for reminding

the city of the sorrows of its brothers'. The play may have been a veiled attack on Athens' foreign policy, but this was still a poor reward for artistic virtuosity. Yet, remembering the volatile temperament of the Greeks, we may forgive those in power for wishing to prevent further contributions to the national despondency.

The audience had a keen sense of their own and their poets' duty to the gods. The burlesqued gods of comedy were pardonable in the spirit of fooling, but anything smacking of a serious attack on religion was strongly disapproved. On one occasion Aeschylus was accused of revealing in a play the secrets of the Eleusinian Mysteries, the most important mystical cult of Greece, whose rites were strictly guarded and divulged only to initiates. A Freemason writing a play about the secrets of his order would meet with the same reception. The audience rose in protest, and Aeschylus was forced to fly for protection to the altar of Dionysus. Public anger was only appeased when Aeschylus proved that he himself was not an initiate, so that if he had sinned, he had sinned without knowledge.

Euripides offended his audience's religious susceptibilities on more than one occasion. One of his characters spoke the notorious line, 'What's shameful when the doer finds no shame?' This was immediately taken as a defence of immorality. Uproar broke out, and the play was only allowed to proceed after explanations had been given. These demonstrations were extremely disconcerting for the author and his cast. They were sometimes vociferous enough to force the play to be withdrawn altogether in mid-performance.

The audience was equally assertive on matters of

artistic taste. One comic poet after another records the fatal *gaffe* of the actor Hegelochus. He had to say 'After the storm I see a calm'. Unfortunately he gabbled the line and ran the words so closely together that the Greek for 'calm' sounded like the word 'cat'. The audience dissolved into laughter and the story passed into theatrical history. Hegelochus was mocked by the comic poets for years afterwards. On another occasion an actor who entered on the wrong cue was howled off the stage. Poets themselves were highly sensitive to audience criticism. The *Clouds* of Aristophanes satirized the foibles of the fashionable sophistic school of philosophy then making itself strongly felt in the city. It seems to have been too obscure for the public taste and met with a lukewarm reception. This led Aristophanes to rewrite it completely, though it is uncertain whether the revised version was ever performed.

The audience needed not only taste but stamina. Festivals began in the early morning and went on for most of the day, for several days on end. At the City Dionysia a typical day contained three tragedies, a satyr play and a comedy. To sit through these on hard stone seats showed a great deal of interest and devotion. We pampered moderns may feel a sneaking sympathy for the spectator who wanted wings to fly away. The plays themselves were not long. It is a major fault of present-day productions to stretch them out to the length of a modern three-act play. Most tragedies could be performed comfortably in little over an hour and a half, a satyr play in fifty minutes, and a comedy in something nearer to two hours. The audience had the intervals between plays in which to stretch its legs and talk, but these could not have been too long ; there was little time, and the dramatic continuity of a trilogy would have suffered. Seats, as we have seen, were arranged in tiers on a semicircular platform. There was a small charge for admission, but as it was a civic duty to attend, the state paid for those who could not afford it. We still have examples of the small disks issued as tickets. These did not allot individual seats. The benches were divided by gangways into sections, and tickets bore the number of a row in a particular section. This system is still used in Greece and some parts of the Continent. Its great advantage is that rows tend automatically to fill up from the centre outwards, and those who arrive early are not disturbed by late-comers stumbling over their legs to find their seats. The lowest tier, on a level with the orchestra, was reserved for religious and civic dignitaries. This practice also is still followed when the ancient theatres are used to-day. As so often happens, the seats kept for important personages command the worst view in the theatre. Each seat in the lowest tier of the Theatre of Dionysus is inscribed with the name of the official who occupied it. The centre seat belonged to the most important of all, the High Priest of Dionysus, whose festival it was, and impressions in the stone bear witness to the countless thousands who have sat in it since that time. Sockets were provided in the stonework to hold awnings which protected the important spectators from the heat. In some theatres, like Priene and the tiny building at Oropos, these seats were given special prominence by being placed within the orchestra circle itself.

Let us then transport ourselves back in imagination to the first day of the festival in Athens two thousand five hundred years ago. It is a public holiday. Work stops, and the narrow streets are full of citizens, rich and poor alike, thronging towards the Theatre of Dionysus on the slope of the Acropolis. Excitement has been aroused in previous days by the preliminary processions and celebrations. The traditional cart of Dionysus, built like a ship, was drawn through the streets by a band of revellers. Yesterday those of us who were lucky enough to get into the Odeion, the great new square building commissioned by Pericles, which overlooks the Theatre, saw the poets whose plays are to compete, together with their actors and choruses in procession, and heard their subjects announced. Thus we go well primed on what we are to see, and have already been recalling past performances of similar themes and wondering if the new plays will equal or surpass them. High above the Theatre, Athens' proudest temple, the Parthenon, rich with sculptures, stands out in the spring sunshine. The Theatre itself has been swept and made ready. The statue of Dionysus is in its place. On the platform a stage-hand is arranging the little furniture required for the first play. We cross the orchestra and climb the steep gangway to a good seat half way up the hillside. Many of our neighbours have come with cushions — the seats are hard after a morning's sitting. Some have brought food and flasks of wine. The large house which is always taken for rehearsals, and has echoed for weeks past to the sound of noble speeches, is now deserted. Behind the scenes the chorus assembles with its flute-player, and the anxious author gives last-minute instructions to his actors as they are helped into their high boots and heavy masks. They will be sweating freely when they take them off again. One actor tries out his voice in a corner. The vast auditorium is now full, a sea of faces, and a reverent hush falls on the gathering as the procession of state officials enters the orchestra. A preliminary prayer of dedication is offered by the High Priest of Dionysus, and the sharp spring sunlight catches the swirl of incense smoke from the altar. We lean forward in our seats in anxious expectation ; the play is about to begin.

CHAPTER V

EARLY TRAGEDY: AESCHYLUS
AND THE *AGAMEMNON*

ESCHYLUS was born about 525 B.C., and his early
life covered a time of vital importance to Athens
both at home and abroad. In the city itself the
autocratic rule of the tyrants was overthrown and a
democracy established which increased in power and
efficiency throughout his lifetime. The turn of the
century brought Persian invasion, the destruction of much
that was best and most sacred in old Athens, and the
wonderful defeat of the foreign armies by Athens and her
allies. Then followed a period of prosperity and reconstruction in which Athens used tribute collected ostensibly
to prepare against future Persian invasions to build new
monuments and temples to replace those that had been
lost. The arts were cultivated, and the theatre shared in
this renaissance.

Aeschylus won his first victory in 484, and over
eighty titles of his plays are recorded. He was famous
both in Athens and outside — he paid two visits to Sicily
to produce plays in the Theatre of Syracuse, almost as old
as that of Athens itself. As well as writing, he took an
active part in city life, fighting at the battle of Marathon
where his brother lost an arm and his life while clinging
to a Persian ship as it drew off from the shore. In 456, on

his second visit to Sicily, he died, according to tradition, by a ludicrous accident. As he sat by the roadside an eagle flying above with a tortoise in its talons saw the sunshine reflected on his bald head, took it for a stone and dropped the tortoise to crack its shell.

Aeschylus wrote for the theatre when it was first assuming an organized form, and so is credited with introducing many of its typical features. The rich costumes and buskins are said to have been designed by him, and he may also have commissioned the architectural decoration of the wooden *skene* by the painter Agatharchus. He took the leading parts in his own plays, using first one and then, imitating Sophocles, two actors to assist him, and also designed his own choral dances. He is also suggested as the first to have used elaborate stage machinery, though apart from the *ekkyklema* none of this is essential to the performance of his plays, and almost certainly dates from considerably later, when the stone theatre was built. As he was the first dramatist whose plays were officially preserved, tradition identified him with the earliest theatrical times, and credited him with inventions whose real origin were lost in antiquity.

Aeschylus dealt with mighty themes, the relation of man to his gods. How far was man responsible for his own actions, how far compelled by the will of heaven? What happens when sacred commands and human compassion conflict? These were problems as momentous for the Greeks as Free Will and Original Sin are for Christianity. He was particularly fond of showing the consequences of human pride, *hybris*, failure to give the gods their due. A successful man may take too much upon himself and go too far, but the gods are jealous of success and the man in power must walk warily. We have already noted one play on this theme, the *Persians*. This was something of a *pièce d'occasion*. It had considerable topical appeal, rare in Greek tragedy. Produced in 472, it told of the battle of Salamis fought and won eight years before. The auditorium was packed with men who had fought the action. The scene is the Persian capital. A chorus of nobles describes the army that has set out to invade Greece, revelling in an elaborate account of the armaments and grand names of the commanders. King Xerxes was to show himself truly great. Already he had subdued the sea by building a bridge across the wild Hellespont that divided the two continents, and throwing chains into the water in token that the sea-god was his slave. A messenger brings the story of what has really happened. His long speech describes the defeat of Xerxes, the ignominious retreat of his army and their pitiful march across country at the mercy of the weather. At the end of the play Xerxes himself appears with the remnants of his army, dressed in rags. This is the punishment for insolence. The *Persians* was Aeschylus' *Henry V*, a stirring patriotic piece that must have brought the audience cheering to their feet.

The gods of Aeschylus are jealous but on the whole just. In the *Prometheus Bound*, Prometheus, a Titan who stole the secret of fire from the gods as a gift for man, is punished by being bound to a desolate mountain peak. He knows the secret that will topple Zeus from his throne, and refuses to reveal it even under threat of worse punishment. There is little movement in the play ; the action consists entirely of a series of dialogues, with the Sea-god Oceanus, the Oceanids his daughters, who form the chorus, Io, another victim of divine vengeance and Hermes, messenger of the gods. At the end of the play a storm hurls him into Hades. In the sequel, now lost (Shelley's *Prometheus Unbound*, though a work of considerable imagination, is no adequate substitute), it is likely that a reconciliation took place.

The characters in these plays are types rather than individuals. They personify the abstract qualities with which the argument deals. For many of them, though they suffer greatly, we find it hard to feel a human compassion. They are on too high a plane, rarefied and ethical qualities, symbols rather than human beings, and we cannot feel sorry for a symbol. The drama of Aeschylus appeals to the intellect rather than to the emotions. When, on the other hand, a character does appeal to our humanity, as in the *Agamemnon*, he does so more strongly in contrast to the formal pattern against which he is set.

Aeschylus' plays were called 'slices of Homer's rich banquets', and he borrows many of Homer's words and turns of phrase. His style is magnificently ornate ; he loves long, elaborate descriptions and sonorous titles. We have seen this in the *Persians*, where he lists the Persian commanders in the manner of an Old Testament genealogy but with far greater cumulative effect ; he uses proper names here as Milton uses them, rejoicing in their sound. His fondness for resounding phrases and lengthy periphrases sometimes produces unintentionally humorous results, as when he calls dust 'mud's thirsty sister', or fish 'the voiceless children of the undefiled', but what in a weaker poet would be fatal are negligible faults in Aeschylus (compare the eighteenth-century poet Thomson's 'finny people', or 'household feathered people' for chickens). The grandeur of Aeschylus' language suits the grandeur of his themes.

Aristophanes' comedy the *Frogs* ends with a trial between Aeschylus and Euripides, both dead when the play was written, in the Underworld, to decide which was the better poet. The trial is pure farce, and should not be taken too seriously as literary criticism, but the author's sympathies clearly lay with Aeschylus. He was fascinated by the brilliance of Euripides, and knew his work well to satirize it so penetratingly, but in the play gives Aeschylus the prize. The older poet is shown as he appeared to a critical though affectionate eye. His repetitions and pomposities are ridiculed, but he replies, justly, by pointing out the shallowness and superficiality of later tragedy and eloquently defends his own philosophy. He was never concerned, he says, with anything mean or sordid. His were great themes, calculated to inspire patriotism and make men proud of their achievements. He sang of the great deeds of the past, and from his plays men learnt martial spirit. The magnificence of his work reflected the magnificence of Athens. This claim was just. At the end of the *Frogs* Aeschylus is sent back to earth to set his city to rights. Athens sought from its playwrights not only entertainment but inspiration. From Aeschylus came inspiration on the highest level.

His influence in the theatre outlived his death. By state command authorized texts of his plays were prepared to prevent cutting and interpolation by later actors. Anyone wanting to revive one of these plays instead of presenting work of his own was granted a chorus automatically. Thus the Athenian audiences for years afterwards were able to watch the plays which helped shape their theatre.

THE *AGAMEMNON*

Aeschylus preferred the trilogy form, groups of three plays linked by a common theme but each complete in itself. This gave the poet a chance to develop his arguments at greater length by presenting different aspects of the basic problem. Trilogies commonly dealt with the fortunes of one house, the working of fate on successive generations. The *Agamemnon* is the first play of the only complete trilogy we have. It was followed by the *Choephoroi* and the *Eumenides*; the three were collectively known as the 'Oresteia' (Orestes-story).

The subject of the 'Oresteia' is the misfortunes of the house of Atreus, King of Argos. Atreus had a brother, Thyestes, whom he suspected of plotting against the throne and banished. Thyestes eventually returned as a suppliant under religious protection. Atreus was unable to do him any personal injury. He pretended to welcome him, but secretly devised a plot. He had Thyestes' children killed and cooked, and served them to their father at a banquet. When Thyestes realized what had happened he cursed the whole house of Atreus. This is the background to the plays, and Aeschylus could assume a knowledge of it in his audience. The trilogy is concerned with the three stages in the working of the curse and its final expiation.

The stage and orchestra are empty. Through a door in the *skene* the watchman enters, and takes up his position ready to speak the prologue. This normally serves two purposes : it establishes the setting of the play and indicates the course of the ensuing action. So the Watchman tells us within a few lines that it is night, and we are before the palace of Agamemnon, Atreus' son. He has been watching a whole year for the signal fire that will announce the fall of Troy. His speech is full of weariness and boredom ; it epitomizes the feelings of a city waiting without news for ten years while its king and menfolk are away at war. Then comes the first mention of Clytemnestra, Agamemnon's queen. It is ominous — 'a woman with a man's resolve at heart'. Suddenly he points ; he can see the beacon, and the audience in their imagination see it too. His fatigue drops from him, his voice rises to a note of joy ; all will now be well, there will be singing and dancing, for the King is coming home. So the Watchman enters the palace to tell Clytemnestra the glad news, but not without a final hint that things have gone badly in Agamemnon's absence :

> These walls, were they but given mouths
> Could tell a tale ; but as for me, I speak
> To those that know — to others, hold my peace.

So time, setting and atmosphere are established with consummate skill in one short speech. The Watchman will not appear again, and retires to change his mask and costume to enter as the Herald later in the play.

Off stage the sound of a flute is heard, and with halting steps the chorus file up the *parodos* and into the orchestra. They are dressed as old men, and each carries a staff. Turning to the audience, they begin an indictment of the follies and miseries of the war that has passed them by.

> We were too old to fight, too old to serve with the others,
> Too few, and they wanted more ; but no-one wanted the old
>   men,

Forgotten in an empty town, our weakness propped on crutches.
Youth and age are alike ; when the sap runs green in the body
Weak limbs are deaf to the call of war ; with winter's coming
We use three legs to walk, weak as a new-born babe,
Wandering through the streets like a dream abroad by daylight.

They sing of a tragic incident that had occurred ten years before. When the combined Greek fleet under the command of Agamemnon and his brother Menelaus sailed for Troy, it was held up at Aulis by contrary winds.

Hungry idleness enchained our ships
By Chalcis' shore in the land of Aulis,
Mocked by the roaring tides that come and go.
Gales swept in from the Strymon, forcing
The men, unwilling to take their ease,
Holding them hungry in the harbour,
Wearing them out with lounging on the shore,
Watching the cables rot and the ships take water,
Adding months to their time away from home,
Wasting their precious strength in doing nothing.

Calchas the seer told Agamemnon that the gods would only let the fleet proceed if appeased by a human sacrifice — the sacrifice of the King's own daughter, Iphigeneia. This is one of those moral problems beloved of Greek tragedy. It was used alone as a theme for other plays. Which was Agamemnon to choose, his family or his command ? He chose the latter. Already the curse of Thyestes was working. Iphigeneia was sacrificed to set the fleet free.

She prayed, called 'Father' ; not all her tears
Nor yet her young virginity could move
Those men of blood to pity. Offering prayer
He signalled those about her as she clung
Half fainting to his robes, to hold her fast
And lift her like a kid above the altar, checking

> With brutal gag the words that, had they fallen,
> Would bring a curse upon her father's house.
> So hung she silent as one painted in a picture,
> Then slowly dropped her garments to the ground
> And turned her timid eyes on those who stood
> Around the altar to assist the sacrifice ;
> For often, when her father's hall was gay
> With feast and laughter had she sung to them,
> Raising her maiden voice in purest song
> As thrice her father poured the gods their wine.

As they sing the central doors of the *skene*, for now
Agamemnon's palace, slowly open. Clytemnestra appears;
she advances to the altar and stands silent as in prayer.
Her silence, its effect increased by the impassive mask,
strikes a sinister note. What is she thinking ? The chorus
wheel round to address her ; it is right, they say, to
honour the Queen in the King's absence. Throughout
the play Aeschylus keeps this reversal of the male and
female rôle before our eyes — things are not as they should
be, the world is upside down. Clytemnestra tells them
with pride of the beacon's journey from Troy to Argos.
Her messenger was

> Hephaestus, his beams piercing the night from Ida's lonely
> summit,
> And beacon fired off beacon as the herald flame spread on
> To Hermes' crag in Lemnos ; then Zeus' home, mountain of
> Athos,
> Snatched up the torch as third in the race ; on it soared sea-
> ward
> Luring the darting shoals to skim the waves in rapture.
> Falling like the glow of sunrise on the sleepless watchers of
> Macestos,
> Who delayed not a moment, but sent it on ; then far away
> by Euripus
> There by its golden light Messapion knew it had come.

Kindled an answering blaze of dry heath ; on it flew, ever
    onward,
Nor did the beacon wane, but like the rising moon
Shone still vigorous over the plain, and came to Cithaeron.
There a new relay awoke ; the guard did not reject it
But burnt more fiercely than was commanded. So it swept
    down
Over the Gorgon-eyed lake to the mountain where the goats
    wander,
Bidding them burn, and burn ; and they ungrudging flung
A mighty beard of flame to the cape that crowns the Saronic
    gulf.
So it swept down, lower still, to alight on the plain of
    Arachnae
Where Argos' neighbour watches ; so came here,
True offspring of the fire of Ida.

This speech is a dramatist's *tour de force* ; it is yet another
example of Aeschylus' fondness for piling name on name.
At first incredulous, the chorus end by rejoicing. Clytemnestra reflects bitterly on the fortunes of war, putting the
view of the losing side :

When you pour oil and vinegar together
In the same vessel, you would call them enemies,
Fighting against each other. So is it now in Troy.
Here shouts of triumph, here low cries of misery,
Voices of the fates that have fallen to either side.
The conquered huddle sobbing in the dust to mourn
A husband's or a brother's stiffened body ; parents keen
Over their children, and from their captive throat
Rises a wild lament for the death of those they loved.

Aeschylus has established two currents of feeling.
Superficially everything is happy — the war is over,
Agamemnon is coming home. But the audience is
conscious of a deeper uneasiness which breaks through in
the Watchman's hints, the sad songs of the chorus and

Clytemnestra's bitterness. The army, though victorious, must still face the dangers of the journey home. Clytemnestra makes her exit, leaving the chorus to sing a song of thanksgiving. They praise Zeus the Saviour for punishing the man who stole Menelaus' wife, and so began the war. They sing of Helen's desertion and echo the Watchman's warnings of trouble. What had once been men were coming back to Argos.

Ares, that stern banker who coins in human blood,
In whose implacable balance the spear-fought battle hangs,
Sends home a heavy load from Troy, fire-tried and cooled in
    tears.
Each of these urns was once a man ; they take up less space
    now
Carrying ashes, an easy load ; the folk weep over them
Remembering the grace that each possessed — a warrior here,
This one well fallen — for another's wife.
No words as yet, but murmuring, sullen resentment
Against the Atreidae who began the war.
Others lie by the wall, cut off in their prime, and laid
In tombs of Trojan earth ; they have won the land they
    fought for.

Though the Greeks have won, Agamemnon must beware. The gods are jealous of success and the pride that goes with it.

The people's blood is up, their talk is dangerous.
Evil forebodings fill my troubled mind.
The man of blood is noted down in heaven.
When he grows rich and offers to neglect
Justice and right, the Furies wear him down
With sorrow piled on sorrow, till he is no more
Than a shadow of himself ; when he is down
There is no man can lift him up again.
Much praise is dangerous, for Zeus is a jealous god
And hurls his lightning down upon the offender.

> I choose the middle way, not to destroy
> Another's city, nor to see my own destroyed.
> Myself made captive and my life dismayed.

Moderation in all things was the abiding tenet of Greek philosophy.

A new character enters. Even if he were not announced by the chorus, his olive-wreath would reveal him as a herald. He brings bad news of the returning army. In realistic terms this is impossible ; the Herald has taken little longer to arrive from Troy than the beacon. But this sort of criticism is out of place in the imaginative drama. The poet is free to subordinate accuracy of time to dramatic fitness ; he compresses episodes that would in reality extend over several days into one continuous dramatic narrative. Perhaps the preceding chorus fulfils the same purpose as the interval in a modern play, and indicates the passage of time. At any rate there is nothing startling in such freedom, and we have many examples nearer home — compare Shakespeare's compression of the French wars in *King John*.

The Herald has three of the best speeches in the play. First, a moving address to his homeland, which echoes the sentiments of every soldier who has ever come back safe from war :

> Dear soil of Argos, land of my fathers, hail !
> Ten years away, this day has brought me home.
> One hope survives of all my shattered dreams —
> Never did I think to die on Argive soil,
> Die and be buried here, my dearest wish.

He reports the King's triumph and impending return. There is a further digression on the horrors of war. Like all old soldiers he is anxious to tell what he has been through.

> Were I to tell you of the hardships we endured,
> Our miserable quarters and the narrow gangways where
> We huddled down to sleep ; there was nothing here
> To give us pleasure. Then when we came to land
> We supped our fill of sorrow — our beds were set
> Under the Trojan walls, from field and sky alike
> Exposed to dews that drizzled on us constantly
> Till our clothes were swarming with vermin.
> Were I to tell
> Of snow that brought intolerable cold and killed
> The birds on the wing, or the parching heat of noon
> When the sea lay motionless without a breath
> To stir it . . .'

Clytemnestra, in a speech full of protestations of love
for her husband, but once more charged with sinister
undertones, orders the Herald to tell him to hasten
his return.

> What day more happy in a woman's life
> Than when her husband comes home safe from war
> To find her at the gates to welcome him ?

she cries, and challenges the chorus to say that she has been
unfaithful in Agamemnon's absence. Alone with the
chorus, the Herald unwillingly reports another disaster.
Menelaus and his ships are missing in a storm :

> The waves rose menacing, and from the Thracian shore
> Fierce strident blasts blew all the ships together,
> And they, encompassed by the fury of the storm
> And the rain that drummed incessantly upon the decks,
> Vanished from sight, a lost and hopeless flock
> Lashed by a madman shepherd.

Note the implications of this narrative. Agamemnon is
now alone, separated from his allies by the will of provi-
dence. The chorus begin their third song, a hymn of hate

against Helen and her fatal beauty.   She is compared to a
wild beast biting the hand that fed it :

> So once a man conveyed a lion cub
> That had but lately learnt its mother's breast
> Out of the forest, and brought it to his home.
> At first its age was tender, loving, kind ; it sported
> Among the children harmlessly, and made
> Their elders laugh to see them play together.
> They could scarce leave it, but every little while
> Would snatch it up to cradle it in their arms,
> While the beast's bright eyes looked for the hand that fed it
> And learnt that fondness brought its food the faster.
> Years passed, and its parents grew within it.
> So it became an unbidden guest
> In its foster home, and brought to the feast
> The husbandman's flock, all slaughtered and torn.
> Everywhere blood ; panic ran through the house
> Without help, without hope ; many lost their lives.
> So God had willed that the lion be reared
> To sacrifice as the priest of Ate.
> She came at first like the calm of summer,
> Gentle and trusting, a precious toy
> With beauty that sent an arrow to the heart.
> A flower with the breath of desire,
> Beginning sweet as the end was bitter.
> She battened upon the sons of Priam,
> Binding them close like an evil spirit,
> A fiend from Hell in the form of a woman
> Sent by Zeus that men might die.

These verses have special significance when we remember
that Helen was Clytemnestra's sister.

The chorus concludes with another warning that
success and wealth are insufficient without goodness :

> Justice shines in sooty dwellings
> Loving the righteous way of life,
> But passes by with averted eyes

> The house whose lord has hands unclean,
> Be it built throughout of gold.
> Caring naught for the weight of praise
> Heaped upon wealth by the vain, but turning
> All alike to its proper end.

Now the theatre is gay with pageantry. Into the orchestra
sweeps a chariot carrying Agamemnon, magnificent in his
robes and flushed with conquest. Behind him march a
few retainers, and the chorus sing a song of welcome as
the procession winds round the orchestra and comes to rest
by the steps. Yet by its very contrast with the previous
solemnity this display frightens us still more. We have
heard over and over again that the gods are jealous of
success, and is not Agamemnon success personified ? We
have heard that justice despises 'the house whose lord has
hands unclean', and are not Agamemnon's hands stained
by the sacrifice of his daughter ? The victorious King
enters his city in triumph ; but the city is empty of all
but old men, the people are resentful, his wife is angry, his
friends have been lost in the storm. For all his success
Agamemnon is isolated and defenceless, and fate's dice are
loaded against him.

He addresses a proud speech to the chorus, and is
in turn addressed by Clytemnestra who comes out to
welcome him. It is a strange speech of welcome, on the
surface full of love and praise ; but she talks across Agamemnon rather than to him, addressing the chorus over
his head as she stands on the platform before the central
doors and he in his chariot beneath her.

> How shall I call my lord, how honour him ?
> The watchdog of the house, the ship's strong mast,
> The grounded pillar binding roof to earth.
> As a father looks upon his only son,

> As storm-tossed sailors on a sudden shore,
> As thirsty travellers in the wilderness
> Upon a flowing stream, so now should Argos
> Look upon Agamemnon.

She apologizes for the absence of their son, Orestes, who has been sent away to Phocis for safety. So Agamemnon is alone with the mother of the girl he has killed. Yet nothing in her behaviour leads him to suspect danger. Only the audience, who know the story, shudder at the dramatic irony of Clytemnestra's concluding words :

> As for the rest, our fitting care shall guide
> With Zeus's aid, the course of things aright.

They know what the course of things is to be.

We may pause here to notice the one touch of humanity Aeschylus has introduced into his portrait of Clytemnestra. For most of the play she is the instrument of vengeance, the channel through which divine wrath is to inflict itself on Agamemnon. In one respect she wins our sympathies — her love for her children. It is her love for Iphigeneia that leads her to destroy her husband, her love for Orestes that makes her send him away when it would be more prudent to kill him too. Ironically, it is this human weakness that brings retribution upon her in the sequel. Aeschylus emphasizes this aspect of her character in the language that she uses ; from her first entrance her speeches are full of mother-imagery.

She lures her husband to his destruction by playing on his vanity. Turning to the palace, she calls her maids. They bring out rich purple tapestries and spread them up the steps from the chariot to the door, a splendid, sinister burst of colour, a ceremonial carpet on which the King must walk. The earth, she hints, is not good enough for the foot of a conqueror. Agamemnon objects horrified. Such stuff is good for gods, not men, to walk on. She persuades him, using all her woman's wiles, arguing that his fame sets him beyond envy. At last he gives in, and steps down from the chariot. In doing so he reveals another figure seated beside him, a woman huddled silently in an attitude of misery. It is a masterly *coup de théâtre* that at Agamemnon's greatest moment of glory this tragic figure should be revealed like a skeleton at the feast. She does not move or speak, and no-one speaks to her. Her brooding ominous presence is a visible expression of the sense of uneasiness that has mounted throughout the first half of the play. She strikes a jarring note at this triumphant homecoming. Agamemnon refers to her as a prisoner of war, and casually tells his wife to treat her kindly.

So Agamemnon enters the palace over the purple carpet, both the culmination and the visible expression of his *hybris*. From this moment his doom is sealed. Clytemnestra remains to make a final prayer at the altar :

Zeus, Zeus, that bringeth all things to pass, hear my prayer
And give due thought to what thou dost intend.

She follows her husband into the house, leaving the chorus, the chariot and the silent prisoner in the orchestra. The premonition of disaster has become a vivid fear :

Why does this persistent dread
Flutter within my heart ?
Why does the song of doom, unprompted,
Beat against my troubled brain ?
Why can I not dispel my fears
As a man shakes off a riddling dream ?
Why do they sit enthroned within me,
Keeping trust from its proper seat ?
Time has grown old since the anchors were weighed

And the sand flew up as the cables sang
And the ships set sail for Troy.
The ships have returned, I have seen them myself.
But still my soul within me chants
The lyreless dirge of the Erinyes.
I have no hope to prop my doubts,
The heart's uneasiness rings true.
The voice within us never lies,
The mind is certain of its fears.
And yet do I hope my fears are false,
And my dread is unfulfilled.

Clytemnestra appears again at the door, and for the first time addresses the prisoner by her name. It is Cassandra, the prophetess, daughter of Priam, King of Troy. She takes no notice. 'Can she not understand?' asks the Queen. 'Or is she mad?' There is no time to waste — 'the sheep stand at the hearth, ready for slaughter'. Again no response. Aeschylus uses her silence to increase the suspense. Clytemnestra retires in anger, leaving the chorus to persuade her. Suddenly and dramatically her silence is broken. She raves in prophetic delirium, seeing the palace peopled with the ghosts of victims of past crimes, and prophesies an even greater crime to come, Agamemnon's murder at the hands of his Queen and her lover :

See where the children sit
Beside the house, pale creatures of the twilight,
Slain by their kindred, each one in his hands
Holding a portion of that tender flesh
That served as food, and show for all to see
Their bodies gashed and torn to make a meal
Whereof their father tasted. Hence I say
Some craven lion, wallowing abed
While others went to war, plots dark revenge
Against the King's return, and he who led

> The fleet to Troy's destruction is bewitched
> By that lewd creature's smiling flattery,
> That fiend he calls his wife, and does not see
> What she conspires with evil to perform.

But hint though she may, the chorus cannot understand her. She explains her own tragic circumstances : Apollo fell in love with her, and gave her the gift of prophecy. When she deceived him he could not take it back, but decreed that, though she should always prophesy the truth, no-one would ever believe her. She foretells her own death ; her speech rises to a crescendo of fury as she tears off her prophet's wreaths and tramples them under foot :

> Why do I wear these dismal trappings still
> As if to mock myself — these wreaths,
> This wand of divination ?   Find another
> To burden with your curse, my part is done.
> See where Apollo strips me of my robes
> Who watched me when I wore them laughed to scorn
> By friends who called me beggar.
> Now I must die, the mortal prophet
> Sacrificed to the one above.
> No more my father's altar, but instead
> The block of execution, reeking red
> With blood my sacrifice shall shed.

She turns towards the palace, pausing at the door to speak one of the most beautiful exit speeches ever written :

> Here in the fading light of sun I pray
> That when the avenger comes, he will remember
> There was a slave who died, and pity me
> In taking vengeance for the greater death.
> Man's life is built on sand ; prosperity
> Is but a shadow, while misfortune's hand need brush
> The poor man's slate but once, and it is blank.
> Much greater is this sorrow than the other.

Cassandra moves our compassion more than any other character in the play. Though we cannot condemn Agamemnon, we do not feel for him. He is a symbol, a personification of *hybris*, rather than a flesh-and-blood human being. We feel that when he dies it will be the end of a stage in an argument, not the end of a life. Cassandra is entirely human, the stranger trapped by chance in the web of others' troubles. Her foreignness emphasizes her isolation. Nothing that happens to her can remotely be called her fault. Her suffering has a personal quality that is lacking elsewhere.

The chorus is left alone. Clytemnestra is inside the palace with her victims. Tension mounts. Once more the chorus stresses the value of moderation. No-one could have been more fortunate than Agamemnon. If he is taken, who is safe?

> You have seen a man
> So well beloved of heaven that the gods
> Gave Troy to be his prize. Should this man now
> Requite in blood the deaths that went before
> And by his death in turn appease the shades
> Of those who fell to his sword, who then
> Could boast himself beyond misfortune's reach?'

Hardly have they finished speaking when two screams ring out from behind the closed doors. It is the King crying for help. Murder has been done.

Now comes one of those difficulties to which the Greek theatre was liable by its nature. The chorus are characterized as old men of Argos. We have seen them anxiously questioning Cassandra and being told of Agamemnon's coming death. Now that death has come. What are they going to do? Dramatic considerations suggest that they should at least attempt to intervene, but the playwright was chary of withdrawing his chorus from the orchestra. Alternatively, they could retain their purely formal significance and comment on the murder in the rôle of spectators. Aeschylus attempts a compromise. He gives each member a single line, and makes them debate what they should do — enter the house, or go to rouse the people. For the first time their two functions conflict, and we feel that their presence is a weakness rather than a strength. Their debate is inevitably inconclusive ; they decide that all they can do is wait and see.

But Aeschylus swiftly recaptures the mood of horror. The central door opens and the *ekkyklema* rolls out carrying a grisly tableau — the body of Agamemnon wrapped in his robe, with Cassandra dead beside him, and Clytemnestra gloating over her two victims. The bodies are of course represented by dummies, as one of the actors is needed again at the end of the play. Clytemnestra has dropped all pretence. She stands revealed as a self-confessed murderess, the personification of vengeance. As the chorus recoil before her she glories in her action.

> Much have I said before to suit the moment
> And feel no shame to contradict it now.
> How else should we entrap our seeming friends
> So closely in the meshes of destruction
> That they could not escape ? This trial of strength
> Has long been in my mind, and brings to a head
> The bitter feud of years. Now it has come.

The chorus accuse her and threaten her with exile. She replies with the insolence of one who knows her position to be unassailable. Anger mounts on either side as she

defends the murder on the grounds that Agamemnon
deserved punishment for murdering his own child.

> You dare to threaten me with banishment
> And with the people's curses ! When this man
> Was living, all his crimes could never move you
> To such a show of wrath ; this man, I say,
> Who sacrificed the child of his own flesh,
> Sweet fruit of my travail, to charm the winds
> Away from Thrace. Was it not he whose crimes
> Cried out for exile ? And when I commit a fault
> Will you at once grow stern, and sit
> In judgement over me ? Know this ; I yield
> To greater strength alone — who conquers me
> Shall be my master. But if the gods
> Intend a different ending to the struggle, you
> Shall be taught a lesson, and shall learn,
> Though late, that you should keep a civil tongue.

The chorus blame Helen and the war for their misfortunes,
but Clytemnestra corrects them ; it is not Helen, but the
family curse that is responsible. They ask who will attend
Agamemnon's funeral — a rite of vital importance for the
Greeks, for unless it were properly conducted the dead
man's spirit would know no peace. Clytemnestra gives
a bitter answer.

> This is no care of yours.
> I struck him, I killed him, I shall bury him.
> And there shall be a mourner for him doubtless :
> No weeping slaves but his own child
> Iphigeneia, as she should, shall stand
> With arms outstretched to take her father home
> Where death's sad river flows through weeping fields
> And set a daughter's kiss on his cold brow.

Their mutual defiance is interrupted by the appearance
of a final character, Aegisthus, Clytemnestra's lover, the
'craven lion wallowing abed' of Cassandra's prophecies.

He comes, typically, when the danger is over. He is one
of Thyestes' sons who survived their uncle's cruelty ; he
was banished, but later returned, and in a long, gloating
speech over the two bodies claims credit for planning the
murder.

> Sweet is the day that looks on vengeance done!
> Now can I truly say the avenging gods
> Look down from heaven on our sufferings,
> When I behold this happy spectacle
> Of Agamemnon in the toils of justice . . .
> Though I was not here,
> I set my foot upon my enemy
> By putting all this fatal plan together.

The chorus reprove him angrily for taking pleasure in
such a deed. He is no man, they tell him, to leave the
murder to a woman, who by killing her own husband
has committed an unspeakable crime against human and
divine law.

Aegisthus retorts that he left it to her out of policy,

> Because deceit was clearly woman's part.
> While I was here in long-suspected enmity,

and threatens them with punishment if they resist further.
He will establish himself as king, and leaves them in no
doubt as to the nature of his rule :

> But I will try to use the dead man's wealth
> To rule his country ; he who obeys me not
> Will quickly find a yoke about his neck.
> No barley-fed young trace-horse he — the pangs
> Of gnawing hunger will soon soften him.

The argument mounts to a climax. Aegisthus loses
his temper and turns to call his guard. The old men,
though threatened with death, are determined to fight to
the last — their staves, they say, are their swords. But

Clytemnestra intervenes; she is sated with killing. Enough lives have been lost already, let them take themselves off before they come to harm.

> If I could cry to these afflictions 'Stop!'
> I would most gladly do so, for the demon
> Grinds his hoof hard upon us.

The chorus prepare to leave, with a final bitter exchange with Aegisthus; if only Agamemnon's son Orestes would come home, and revenge his father's death! So, to the sound of the flute, heads bowed in sorrow, the chorus file wearily out of the orchestra. Aegisthus and Clytemnestra, side by side, turn and enter the palace. The *ekkyklema* with its load is withdrawn; the door closes; the stage and orchestra are left empty, and, as the final notes of the flute die away off stage, the play is over.

The second play of the trilogy, the *Choephoroi* (*Libation Bearers*), continues the story of the curse into the next generation. Orestes and his friend Pylades arrive secretly from the Phocian court. While praying by his father's tomb he meets his sister Electra, who has come with a chorus of maidens to make grave offerings. At last they meet, and invoke their dead father's aid. Orestes disguises himself as a foreigner and gains admittance to the palace, where he kills both Clytemnestra and Aegisthus; Cassandra's final prophecy is fulfilled. Yet for this he must himself be punished; he is doomed to be pursued by the Furies, supernatural bringers of retribution. The *Eumenides* gives the end of the story. It opens with Orestes seeking sanctuary in Apollo's shrine at Delphi. Apollo sends him to Athens, where his case will be tried. Clytemnestra's ghost appears, wakes the Furies and sends them after him in hot pursuit. The second half of the play is set in Athens, where Orestes pleads before the Court of the Areopagus. He is acquitted, and the story ends.

A great play is like an onion. The further we penetrate, the more layers of meaning we reveal. Great works of art are appreciable on many levels, and each generation, examining them in the light of its own culture and beliefs, finds something to admire. Superficially, the 'Oresteia' is a violent story of a primitive family feud. So, at its lowest level, is *Hamlet*. But Aeschylus' work, like Shakespeare's, is much more than a tale of revenge. Aspect after aspect reveals itself as we search deeper. One of these, the theological, is now perhaps impossible for us to appreciate fully. Christian beliefs are so far removed from the Greek conception of deity as a jealous power bending men to a preordained fate, that we need a considerable effort of imagination and scholarship to recreate the atmosphere of those times ; even then we cannot do so with conviction. There must inevitably remain something strange and barbarous about the gods of the *Agamemnon*. Yet the moral values are eternally fascinating. Agamemnon was forced to choose between public and private good ; choosing the former, he secured his army's safety by sacrificing his own daughter. Clytemnestra sought vengeance for her child, though it meant killing her husband. Orestes was in duty bound to avenge his father, even at the cost of matricide. In this recurring saga of crime and punishment, who was right and who wrong ? The reader will not find the answers in this book. He must study the plays for himself, with the wealth of commentary that has been written on them. As we have seen, the *Agamemnon* is also a bitter indictment of war. It speaks continually of the folly of bloodshed, of the hardships of fighting, of the misery at home that is the inevitable counterpart of glory in the field. We must remember that it was written by a man who had been a soldier himself, who had seen his brother die and his beloved city laid in ruins. For this message alone the play repays study.

The great dramatic merit of the *Agamemnon* is its simplicity. With a minimum of characters and a bare economy of situation Aeschylus establishes a tension that does not relax until the final word has been spoken, and even then leaves us anxiously awaiting the sequel. The author has seen this well pointed in a modern production of the play where the staging at the end exactly reduplicated the beginning. As Aegisthus and Clytemnestra withdrew, the Watchman appeared and took up the position in which he had spoken the prologue, still watching for a sign of hope, this time not the beacon but the return of Orestes.

Characters are strongly and simply drawn : the Watchman's weariness, the Herald's joy at homecoming, Agamemnon's self-sufficiency, Clytemnestra's cunning and hypocrisy, the jackal's spite of Aegisthus. The narrative is loaded with dramatic irony which yet never obtrudes, only coming to surprise us when we least expect it. The language is rich in metaphor and poetic imagery. Passages already quoted reveal, however inadequately, many of these, but there are hundreds more. Of an impossible hope Aeschylus says, 'A boy might catch a flying bird as easily'. Zeus working the destruction of Troy is 'fastening the net of doom tight around the Trojan turrets'. The wooden horse is 'the fierce beast of Argos with its warrior load'. To know the beauty of

Aeschylus' language the student must read the play in full, if not in Greek, in several translations, for no one is capable of transmitting its complexity.

What we can deduce of the stage production reveals a keen sense of visual effect and the value of simplicity. Clytemnestra aloof in prayer while the chorus sing of the city's troubles ; the brilliant display of Agamemnon's entry after a chorus heavy with sorrow and foreboding ; the silent, ominous figure of Cassandra introducing a discordant note into the triumphant homecoming ; the vivid splash of colour as the purple carpet is spread up the steps — all these argue a great producer as well as a great writer

So the *Agamemnon* illustrates all that was best in the tragedy of its time. Dignified and stately, it moves with the certainty of ritual to a known and preordained conclusion. Lacking surprise, it never lacks interest ; it can still grip a modern audience as it gripped the Athenians who saw it for the first time on a spring day over two thousand years ago.

CHAPTER VI

LATER TRAGEDY: EURIPIDES
AND THE *MEDEA*

EVERY generation produces its 'angry young men', writers and thinkers sensitive to the flaws in existing institutions and making it their duty to expose them. They are the self-appointed critics of the times, declared enemies of complacency, woolly thinking and narrow-mindedness. Such a one was Euripides. If we may call Aeschylus the Marlowe of the Greek theatre — at least the Marlowe of *Faustus* and *Tamburlaine* — then Euripides was its Galsworthy or Shaw, though with more humour than the former and lacking the latter's impish delight in argument for its own sake. Like his modern counterparts, he was fond of revealing the hollowness of current beliefs, of paradox, of demonstrating the logical conclusions of popular theories. All was grist to his mill. He took institutions regarded by the Greeks as sacrosanct, examined them with a merciless eye and presented them on the stage in strange and unpleasant aspects.

Yet to a large extent Euripides was only the child of his time. Sophocles had written the tragedy of Oedipus, the king who fell from the summit of his power to the depths of degradation ; in the last quarter of the fifth century the fortunes of Athens suffered a change equally catastrophic. Her power was based on economic suprem-

acy and her position at the head of a league formed originally as a safeguard against Persia and now transformed into
an Athenian empire.   Under the guidance of her great
statesman Pericles the city prospered, and money coerced
yearly from the confederate states went to great building
projects and elaborate schemes of reconstruction.   Athens'
history reads like the plot of a tragedy.   Her pride and
prosperity increased until she enjoyed a position unique
in the ancient world ; then came the inevitable reaction.
Her supremacy could not be expected to go unchallenged
for long.   Sparta, a strong military state, had been ousted
from her unofficial leadership of Greek cities, and grew
jealous.   Something had to be done to break the economic
stranglehold of the Athenian bloc. Tension slowly mounted,
and in 431, after the usual exchange of pretexts, war was
declared.

Greece was divided against itself.   Sparta led a coali-
tion of powerful cities dissatisfied with Athenian leadership, and Athens opposed them with the full might of her
empire.   Sparta had a strong army with capable leaders,
Athens the greatest fleet of the age.   Interested countries,
Persia and Macedon, watched the struggle from a distance,
flirting first with one side, then with the other as their fortunes veered.   The war began conventionally with a Spartan
army invading Attica to destroy the crops.   Instead of
marching out to fight in the usual way the Athenians
withdrew within their walls.   They refused to waste their
strength in open combat, but carried the war into the
enemy's territory with their fleet.   Overcrowding in the
city caused plague, in which Pericles died.   An uneasy
peace was engineered, but could not last.   Allied states,
weary of Athenian domination, began to revolt, and the

tide of war turned against Athens. An attempt to recoup her fortunes by a costly expedition to Sicily ended in disaster. Mismanagement and suspicion at home were matched by weakness and incompetence at the front. At last, torn internally by revolution and counter-revolution, Athens succumbed after nearly thirty years of war which cost her not only her power, but the distinctive qualities which she had used that power to foster.

The changes in the war caused corresponding changes in the city. When Pericles died Athens fell into the hands of a new class of politician. These were *nouveaux riches*, men of the people, with great skill in swaying the mob but lacking the forethought and restraint necessary for the conduct of the war. Old traditions of dignified statesmanship died out. Men's beliefs too were changing. Visiting orators gave impetus to the study of rhetoric for its own sake. Men learnt that it was the best-presented argument, not always the true one, that carried the day. This art of discussion was fostered by a new school of philosophical teachers, the sophists. Although some, like Socrates, were interested purely in revealing the illogicality of popular conceptions, the inferior sort delighted in twisting facts and proving black to be white. At the same time a new materialism began to attack the values of established religion. Rational scientific inquiry sought to destroy popular beliefs.

So, as the prosperity of Athens declined, scepticism and agnosticism increased. Nothing was secure any longer. If Athens fell, what could be called safe ? It was an age of doubt and disillusion. Yet it was not entirely harmful. Though it lost much in throwing the old order overboard, it gave birth to a new spirit of inquiry. Faced with the destruction of all that had once seemed permanent, men learnt to think for themselves. As always, the stage reflected the conditions of the time, and produced in Euripides a dramatist who was in the forefront of the new movement. The tragedies of Aeschylus and Sophocles had dealt with moral problems, but their treatment of them lay within the framework of the established religion. Sophocles, though far from impervious to the new teachings, kept faith with the past. Euripides set himself outside the established institutions, and criticized them.

Euripides was born in 485. It is difficult to disentangle the facts of his life from unreliable gossip, as he was personally unpopular. His views were too advanced for many of his contemporaries ; he was distrusted, and his habit of writing in solitude gave him a reputation for moroseness. It was a favourite joke of the comic poets to sneer at his lowly origins. His mother was said to have been a greengrocer, though this is probably untrue. Another slander was that his plays were really written by his servant or actor Cephisophon. In the trial scene of the *Frogs* Aeschylus and Euripides are weighing quotations in a balance. Aeschylus suddenly explodes, 'Let him jump in the scales himself, with all his plays, his family and Cephisophon — I'll weigh one of my lines against the lot !'

Euripides set himself to revalue the stories of the gods in the light of human motives and behaviour. To suggest that the divine conduct was not altogether praiseworthy was not new, but it was the first time that popular mythology had been attacked with such deadly logic and concentrated force. Euripides' method is to strip traditional tales of their aura of romance and present them simply as moral problems.

93

'This is how we are told the gods behaved,' he says, 'but if human beings behaved in such a way, should we not condemn them out of hand?' We shall see his contemptuous attitude to popular fairy-tale conceptions in the *Medea*. In the *Bacchantes*, one of his most gruesome plays, we have a picture of a god working all manner of misery on mankind. The scene is Thebes. The new cult of Dionysus has spread like wildfire through the city, and the women are his frenzied devotees. Pentheus, the King, stoutly refuses to conform, and repudiates the divinity of this new god. So Dionysus appears in human form, and leads him on to his destruction. Pentheus makes a vain attempt to imprison his strange visitor but eventually succumbs; he is lured to watch the maddened women performing their wild rites, from the vantage-point of a tree. He is discovered; they mistake him in their frenzy for a wild beast, and tear him apart with their bare hands. Agave, his mother, carries the head in triumph. The horrible scene in which she slowly recovers her sanity, and with it the dreadful realization of what she has done, is one of the most gripping ever written for the theatre. We are left, as Euripides intended, with a feeling of revulsion at the demoniac triumph of the god.

Similarly, in *Hippolytus* the action springs from a divine desire for revenge. Hippolytus is devoted to hunting and to Artemis, Goddess of the Chase. Aphrodite, Goddess of Love, is offended by his neglect, and makes his stepmother Phaedra fall in love with him. Phaedra's guilty passion makes her ill. In a mistaken attempt to help, her old nurse tells Hippolytus the reason. He, an honourable youth, is horrified, and accuses Phaedra in the most scathing terms. Thwarted, she revenges herself by suicide, leaving a note accusing Hippolytus of her death. Theseus, her husband, believes the note and calls down a curse on his son's head. This operates almost immediately ; while driving his chariot on the shore Hippolytus is attacked by a sea-monster and mortally injured. He is carried on to the stage dying, and Aphrodite's triumph is complete.

Euripides' second great theme is the misery of war. It took courage to write such things when Athens was fighting for her life ; but the *Trojan Women* has been described as the greatest anti-war play ever written. It depicts the suffering of the Trojan womenfolk when their husbands have been killed and their city and homes destroyed, as they await whatever fate their conquerors shall decide for them. The *Phoenician Women*, with a cast-list of unique length in Greek tragedy, compresses the whole Theban saga into one play to point the moral that war leads only to evil and destruction. *Hecuba* concentrates on the misfortunes of the erstwhile Queen of Troy. A captive in the Greek tents, she learns the faithlessness of supposed friends and that kindness is too often repaid with injury. Her daughter is sacrificed to appease the ghost of Achilles, and it is Odysseus, whom she had befriended when he entered Troy as a spy, who brings the news. Her son Polydorus was entrusted to a family friend to keep him out of danger ; this friend has killed him for his money. These lessons had particular point ; the Athenians were rapidly finding out what it meant to be on the losing side.

Aeschylus, in the *Frogs*, accuses Euripides of portraying bad women in his plays. It is true that he found great interest in analysing women's characters, and his treatment of many of them is far from sympathetic. Aristophanes' comedy, the *Thesmophoriazusae* (*Mother's Day*), shows the women of Athens up in arms against this unfair treatment. Aeschylus also accuses his rival of preoccupation with the sordid and unworthy. His own plays, he claims, had given the citizens good examples, and inspired them to greater achievements ; those of Euripides could only produce a race of degenerates. Euripides retorts that his main concern is to teach people to think for themselves, and not to take for granted the illogical beliefs foisted on them by past generations. His god is Reason. To find out the truth is everything, no matter how many muck-heaps are stirred up in the process.

Yet even Euripides could have his lighter vein. We have already noted the charming tale of *Helen*, a romantic melodrama with humorously drawn characters and a happy ending. In the *Alcestis*, written instead of the usual satyr play, all works out well in the end. Admetus has been told that he must die unless he can provide Death with a substitute. His wife Alcestis makes the supreme sacrifice and takes his place. Admetus, a wonderful study in unconscious selfishness, accepts her sacrifice while mourning bitterly that she must go. Into this picture of domestic grief comes, heavy-footed, the demi-god Heracles, who accepts Admetus' hospitality and only afterwards discovers what is going on. He is appalled at his own tactlessness, but makes amends by going off to wrestle with Death for the dead wife, triumphantly restoring her to her husband. The play has cynical moments, notably the scene where Admetus accuses his old father of selfishness ; his life is nearly over, why should he not give himself up to die and spare the young ? But in spite of this, the theme is handled lightly and with sophistication and there are deft touches of comedy.

Euripides was a prolific writer. He wrote over ninety plays, of which nineteen have survived. Although too controversial a figure to achieve popularity in his lifetime — he won only five first prizes — his plays were acted long after his death, and more often than those of his two predecessors. His *Bacchantes* was being performed at the Parthian court in 55 B.C., shortly after the defeat of the invading Roman army and their general Crassus. Crassus' head was cut off and rushed post-haste to the court, where it arrived in time to be used at the appropriate point in the play. Many Athenians were shocked by his arguments though attracted by the skill with which he presented them. His posthumous success was due not only to his humanistic approach to moral problems but to the sheer theatrical quality of his work. His plays are written with great force and pungency; they contain memorable scenes rather than finely drawn characters, and have everything to hold an audience's attention.

In the practical field of production Euripides was as original as in his philosophy. The greater realism of his plots demanded a corresponding realism in their presentation. This comes out strongly in his use of the scene-building. For Aeschylus the *skene* had been merely a background for his actors. The fact that it was architecturally decorated did not bind him. He ignored it when he pleased, setting his scenes wherever seemed appropriate and changing their location as the action progressed. If a house or palace was needed, the *skene* could represent it, but if not, it could be conveniently forgotten. Euripides' approach is quite different. The building against which his plays were set looked like a house, and so must be treated as one. He preferred to confine his action to one setting, and let the *skene*'s permanent and unmistakable presence govern the movement of his characters. In Aeschylus the background is dictated by the play, in Euripides the play by the background. Previously the upper storey of the *skene* had conventionally represented the heavens, on which gods might appear. For Euripides it was simply the roof of a house. Characters walk on it and climb over it. In a serio-comic scene in his *Orestes* a cowardly Phrygian escapes from the palace by scrambling over the roof. Later actors, who thought this stage business too dangerous, rewrote the play to allow them to enter through the doors in the usual manner. The action, with rare exceptions, is confined to this one location. In Euripides we have the beginnings of the realistic setting.

Euripides produced his plays himself, with one possible exception, and every one reveals the hand of the born showman. He delighted in effects for their theatrical value, apart from their relevance to the plot. To him may be attributed the development of the *mechane*, to represent characters flying ; Aristophanes satirizes it as a particularly Euripidean device. He frequently uses processions and elaborate ceremonial entrances — the *Suppliant Women* has two funeral cortèges, and the second, with a procession of sons carrying the ashes of their dead fathers, must have had an overwhelming effect. *Coups de théâtre* are many. In the *Trojan Women* the body of the child Astyanax is brought in on his dead father's shield, and Andromache makes her entrance in a humble mule-cart, a pathetic contrast to the pomp and dignity normally accompanying the appearance of stage princesses. We have already seen his taste for bizarre effects in the *Bacchantes*, with its chorus of frenzied, drum-beating women and grisly scene with Pentheus' head. Foreign settings and characters are used for their exotic value — the Egyptian background of *Helen*, the Phrygian in *Orestes*, the barbaric Thracian soldiers in *Hecuba*. In costume also Euripides permitted himself greater realism than was customary. In the *Acharnians* of Aristophanes, Dicaeopolis, an elderly Athenian, is forced to defend his conduct before an indignant and hostile chorus. To give his plea greater pathos he decides to dress the part, and goes to borrow suitable clothes from Euripides. The poet lends him the costume of one of his typical tragic heroes — a dress of rags, an old cap and a staff. With their assistance Dicaeopolis is able to present himself as the picture of misery.

Euripides attacked the theatre like a new broom, brushing old conventions aside, making innovations which at the time were daring and original, and revolutionizing the conception of the stage setting. Much of what he despised was valuable. We miss the unique combination of grandeur and flexibility that the theatre enjoyed under Aeschylus and Sophocles. Yet his freshness of approach gave new power to the art-form by turning it into new paths more appropriate to current thought. Aeschylus in the *Frogs* claims that Euripides has him at a disadvantage in the underworld because 'my plays have not died with me, as his have'. Aeschylus was wrong. For their theatrical qualities alone Euripides' plays have won a deserved reputation. Aeschylus would have done better to apply his criticism to Euripides' successors. When he died, Greek tragedy died with him.

THE *MEDEA*

The well-known legend on which this play is based tells how Jason sailed with a band of heroes in the magic ship, the *Argo*, to find the fabulous Golden Fleece, the property of the King of Colchis. The King's daughter, Medea, fell in love with him and used her knowledge of witchcraft to surmount the formidable obstacles in his way. They left together, Medea sacrificing her own brother to delay pursuit. Returning to Jason's city of Iolkos, she tricked the King's daughters into killing their father by teaching them a magic process which she said would restore his youth. Instead, he died in anguish. Jason and Medea then went to Corinth, where the play is set. Euripides follows his usual practice of stripping the story of its glamour and concentrating on the sordid aftermath. Jason wishes to secure his position by making an advantageous marriage with the daughter of King Creon, though this means abandoning Medea and her children. It is here that the play opens.

Medea's old nurse appears to speak the prologue. She tells of her mistress's betrayal, and her present unhappy situation. In losing her husband's love she has lost everything.

> Everything she did was for Jason's sake,
> And that's the best way of avoiding risks,
> For a wife to have no difference with her husband.
> But love is dying, and there's hatred everywhere.

Jason betrays my mistress and his children
To make a royal alliance, marrying
The daughter of Creon, ruler of this land.
While Medea is left wretched and dishonoured
To cry 'You promised !' and remind him of the hand
He pledged in faith, and calls on heaven to see
What she has done for him, and her reward.
She lies without eating, abandoned to her grief,
Weeping herself thinner with each day that passes
Since first she knew her husband was unfaithful.
Never raising her eyes, or lifting her face
From the ground, deaf as rock or water
To anyone who gives her good advice. . . .
Poor lady, she has come to learn the hard way
What it means to have no country to go back to.
She hates her children, takes no pleasure in seeing
      them ;
I'm afraid she has something dreadful in her mind.
She's a dangerous woman — who makes an enemy
Of her won't come off victor easily.

So the prologue strikes the familiar note of impending
disaster.   Now the children themselves appear with their
tutor, a typical Euripidean figure, a cynic who accepts the
ways of the world with a resigned shrug.   That a husband
can be faithless is no surprise to him.   The children stand
silent while he relates some malicious gossip :

I heard somebody saying, and pretended not to listen,
When I was at the place where the old men sit
Playing draughts around the holy fountain of Peirene,
That Creon, ruler of this country, was about
To send the children with their mother into exile
Away from Corinth.

So Medea is to lose her home as well as her husband.   The
Nurse, shocked at this new example of man's perfidy,
packs the children off inside the house.   Medea's voice

rings out from behind the scenes, lamenting her mis-
fortune. She chants the bitter story of her desertion, and
wishes that she may die. The chorus enters ; they represent women of Corinth, drawn by her cries to approach
the palace. Sympathetic but resigned, they are prepared
to offer consolation :

> I heard the voice, I heard the cry
> Of Colchis' unhappy daughter.
> It is ringing still. Tell us, old woman.
> I was inside at my door, and heard her crying.
> I cannot be happy when the home is troubled,
> When the home is one I love.
>
> Zeus, heaven and earth, do you hear
> How the wretched wife is weeping ?
> What makes you long for that dreadful sleep ?
> Fool, would you wish your death sooner ?
> This is no way to pray. If your husband
> Honours another wife, it has happened
> To others. Don't take it to heart.
> Zeus will see justice done, don't wear
> Yourself out with lamenting your husband.

At last the doors open and Medea appears. One of Aeschylus' favourite tricks was to leave a character silent on the
stage for some time, to rouse the audience's interest — we
have seen how he did this with Cassandra. Euripides,
equally effectively, uses the trick of the delayed entrance.
We have heard her voice, we have watched the chorus
and Nurse discussing her, but have not yet seen her :
her appearance, when it comes, is thus doubly effective.
Again like Cassandra, her isolation is emphasized by the
fact that she is a foreigner. This would not be apparent
from her voice — that sort of realism is found only in
comedy, where characters frequently use dialect — but

we may be sure that Euripides, with his love of the exotic, would have stressed the foreign element in her costume. Contemporary vase paintings illustrating the play indicate as much. She is a strange, slightly barbaric figure, a stranger from the borders of the known Greek world. Euripides partially vindicates himself from the charge of portraying bad women by putting into her mouth a statement, bitterly true, of their position in the social structure. They have no rights, no privileges ; a man may do as he pleases, but women have only the prospect of a dull, monotonous, confined existence :

> Of all things living that possess a mind,
> We women are the most unfortunate.
> First we must put ourselves to vast expense
> To buy a husband, and take a master for
> Our bodies — a worse evil than the other.
> And everything depends on whether we take a good man
> Or a bad one ; divorce is not respectable
> For women, we cannot repudiate our husbands.
> Coming to new manners and a new way of life
> She needs second sight to know how best to manage
> Her bedfellow — nobody taught her at home.
> And if we work hard at it, and our husband
> Lives with us without struggling against the yoke,
> We are to be envied. If not, there is death.
> When a man is bored with the people in his household
> He can go out to find his consolation,
> But we have only one soul-mate to look to.
> They tell us we can spend our lives in safety
> At home, while they go out to fight the wars.
> How illogical ! I'd rather stand three times
> In the battlefield than bear one child.

As the chorus stand silent before her eloquence, she appeals to them to help her. If she finds some way to revenge herself on her husband for this injury, they must promise not to give her away. In the plays of intrigue such as this, the constant presence of a chorus is a particular drawback. The artificiality of the convention at once becomes obvious, especially under Euripides' realistic treatment. Aeschylus accepts his medium and works within its limitations, but Euripides sometimes gives the impression of fighting against them, trying to pack into the tragic framework more than it can bear. One would expect Medea to contrive her plots in secret, but the chorus, always present, must be confided in, and so remain uneasy spectators of the outcome.

Creon, the King, appears, to confirm the Tutor's suspicions. Medea must go into exile. He is disarmingly honest, and makes no attempt to conceal his motives. When Medea asks indignantly how she has deserved this punishment, he replies :

> I am afraid of you. Why cloak my words ?
> Afraid you will do my child some fatal hurt.
> And many things contribute to my fear —
> You are clever, and accomplished in black arts,
> And angry that your husband has deserted you.
> You threaten, so I hear from my informers,
> To do something to the bridegroom and the bride,
> And her father too. I would rather be safe than sorry.
> Better be hated, woman, by you now,
> Than weaken, and repent my weakness later.

Medea deplores the fate of the individualist in a speech which might well refer to Euripides' own position. Nothing is more dangerous than a reputation for cleverness.

> This has happened before. It is not the first time, Creon,
> I have been the victim of my reputation.
> No sensible man should ever have his sons
> Brought up more clever than the common run.

Apart from being told they waste their time,
They earn the spite and envy of their neighbours.
You'll be called good-for-nothing, not intelligent,
For holding unconventional ideas.
And if the know-alls find your reputation
Exceeding theirs, the state will turn against you.

It is a sentiment strikingly modern in its application ; it
was to become more and more relevant to Athens in the
years following the production of *Medea*. Socrates, the
greatest free-thinker of his time, was to die for his beliefs.

Creon is unmoved. Medea urges him by every possible plea ; she flings herself at his feet in supplication,
while he stands with his impassive mask turned away from
her in a gesture of rejection. At last she wrings from him
one reluctant concession. Although her banishment is
irrevocable, Creon allows her one day's grace to make
arrangements for her journey and find somewhere to go.
He acts against his better judgement. He has been stern,
but is no tyrant. He is presented throughout as a simple
man whose family comes first in his affections. With all
the simple man's distrust of what is new and strange, he
fears this foreigner and is alive to the dangers of allowing
her to remain in his country. His humanity is to prove
his undoing. Plainly uneasy, he goes out, persuading
himself that a day is too short for Medea to do any
harm.

Yet a day is all she needs. No sooner has Creon gone
than she changes from the cringing suppliant to the
sorceress. She reveals her plan to the chorus. Jason and
his new bride must die — but how ? If she can find some
friend to take her in and protect her from subsequent
reprisals, she will poison them and escape, but in the last
resort she will kill them with her own hands and face the

consequence. She prays to the dark spirit of witchcraft, reminding us of her divine ancestry :

> No, by the Queen of Night, whom above all
> I honour and have chosen for my partner,
> Hecate, whose home is in the corners of my hearth,
> No man shall break my heart and still live happy.
> I will make them weep and curse the day they married,
> Curse this alliance and my banishment.
> Then come, Medea, call on all the skill
> You have in plotting and contriving.
> On to the crime. Now comes the test of courage.
> Look to your wrongs. You must not let yourself
> Be mocked by Jason's Sisyphean wedding,
> You, a royal child, descended from the Sun,
> You have the skill ; moreover, you were born
> A woman ; women are incapable of good,
> But have no equal in contriving harm.

The chorus reply with a lament for their own sex. Who can now accuse women of lying and deceit, when men behave as Jason has to Medea ?

> The sacred rivers flow back to their sources,
> The appointed order of things is reversed.
> It is men whose minds are deceitful, who take
> The names of their gods in vain,
> And women the future will honour in story
> As leaders of upright lives.
> Glory is ours ! and the slanderous tongues
> That attacked womankind shall be stilled.
>
> You Muses of past generations, inspire
> No more the refrain that women are fickle.
> We were not granted the wit by Phoebus
> Apollo, the master of songs,
> To strike from the lyre its heavenly music.
> If it were so, I should sing
> In answer to men ; for history tells
> As much of men's lives as of ours.

Jason enters. Euripides has already built up a prejudice against him in our minds before he even begins to speak. We have seen his conduct through the eyes of his victim and of a partial observer, the Nurse. How can he attempt to justify himself? It soon becomes clear that he is guiltless in his own eyes. He is prepared to justify his second marriage on grounds of policy, and blames the rest on Medea herself. He is arrogantly self-righteous. How can she expect to be well treated when she criticizes the actions of her betters? If she had kept quiet, all would be well. This arrogance would be insufferable if it were not for the fact that Jason honestly believes what he is saying. He is not attempting to lie and excuse himself. What he has done is advantageous for himself, and so must be right. In offering Medea money to support her in her banishment he considers that he has discharged his obligations. The other considerations — love, trust, honour — he does not take into account. So the romantic hero of legend is shown as selfish and unfeeling. Medea reacts forcibly to this declaration. She reminds him of all she has done for his sake :

> I saved your life, as every single Greek
> Who sailed with you on board the Argo knows,
> When you were sent to tame the bulls that breathed
> Flames, and yoke them, and sow death in the field.
> The dragon who encircled with his coils
> The Golden Fleece, and watched it without sleeping,
> I killed for you, and lit your road to safety.
> And I betrayed my father and my home
> To sail to Iolkos and Mount Pelion
> With you, and showed more eagerness than sense.
> I brought on Pelias the worst of ends,
> Death at his children's hands, and ruined his house.
> All this I accomplished for your worthless sake,

> To be abandoned for another woman
> Though I had borne your sons ! If you were childless,
> You might have some excuse to marry again. . . .
> Where shall I turn now ? To my father's home,
> The country I betrayed to come with you,
> Or Pelias' wretched daughters ? They would give
> A gracious welcome to their father's murderess.
> For that is how it is. I have estranged
> Myself from friends at home, and those I should
> Not wrong I have made mortal enemies for your sake.
> In recompense how happy have you made me
> Among Greek women ! What a paragon
> Of rectitude I married, to my sorrow,
> When I am exiled, thrown out of the country
> Without a friend. My sons are all I have.

Jason is amazed at her ingratitude. Has she not profited handsomely from their association ? She saved his life, it is true, but the Goddess of Love should really have the credit for this. If she had not inspired Medea with a passion for Jason, it would never have happened. Let Medea count her blessings.

> To begin with, instead of living among savages,
> You live in Greece, and have come to learn our justice
> And how to live by laws and not brute force.
> What's more, all Greece has heard how clever you are.
> You're famous. If you still lived at the ends
> Of the earth, nobody would have heard of you.

It does not occur to him that Medea's reputation has proved the reverse of advantageous, or that his present behaviour is not a shining example of Greek justice. But women, says Jason, are so unreasonable. They cannot tell what is good for them. If their husband wants to take a new wife, they think the world has come to an end. So Medea and Jason leave their long speeches of defiance and fall to a harsh squabble. Jason loses patience. His second

offer of money refused, he leaves his wife to her own
devices and stamps off angrily to the palace, pursued by
Medea's angry taunts.

The chorus sing of the mixed blessings of Love, stress-
ing the favourite Greek maxim that moderation is best.

> Love unrestrained can bring
> A man no worth or honour,
> But coming in small measure
> There is no power more gracious.
> Never let fly at me,
> Great Queen, the unerring shafts
> Of your golden arrows, dipped
> In the poison of desire.
>
> Let moderation be
> My shield, God's finest gift.
> Dread Aphrodite, never
> Send strife and argument
> To attack my heart and make
> Me long for other loves,
> But learn to honour marriage
> And let love lie at peace.

An old man appears on the stage. That he is a king, and
travelling, is apparent from his costume. He is Aegeus,
King of Athens, and addresses Medea kindly. This is the
very protection Medea is looking for. Throwing herself
on his mercy, she tells him her story, and begs him to
shelter her. Aegeus is willing, though cautious :

> This is how I stand. If you reach my country,
> I'll try to befriend you as in duty bound.
> But one thing I must make clear from the start,
> I'm not prepared to get you out of Corinth.
> If you can make your own way to my home,
> You may have sanctuary, I'll give you up to no-one.
> But you must make your own escape from the country.
> I do not wish to give offence, even to strangers.

This scene, though effective, is inconsistent. Euripides makes Aegeus speak as though he were aware of what Medea is about to do. But up to this point no-one knows her intentions but the chorus. Aegeus' scruples seem odd when we consider that, far from wishing to prevent her leaving the country, the authorities are only too glad to be rid of her. Aegeus and Medea talk as if the coming murder were known to both of them. But this is a minor blemish. Aegeus swears an oath to befriend her ; now she is certain of her refuge, and can proceed with her plan. When he goes, commended by the chorus for his kindness, she tells in greater detail what she means to do — send her sons with presents to the princess, a robe and golden diadem. They will be impregnated with deadly poison, so that she and all who touch her will die in agony. One thing then remains for her to do :

> I will kill my children,
> My sons ; no man shall take them from me.
> And when the house of Jason lies in ruins
> I will leave the country, putting my darlings' death
> Behind me, an offence that stinks to heaven,
> The scorn of enemies is unendurable.
> Let it go ; what can I hope from life ? I have
> No home, no country, no escape from misery.
> I made my mistake the day I left behind
> My father's house, seduced by speeches from
> A Greek who heaven knows will pay for them.
> The sons I bore him he will never see
> Alive after this day, or father more
> On his new-married bride, condemned to die
> In agony from my poison as she deserves.
> No-one shall call me timorous or weak
> Or stay-at-home, but quite the opposite.
> A menace to my enemies and help to friends.
> They are the people that the world remembers !

The chorus are horrified at this dreadful decision. In an effort to dissuade her they sing the lovely ode to the glories of Athens (quoted in Chapter IV). How, they ask, will a city standing for truth and justice give sanctuary to a murderess? Medea is unmoved. She has sent again for Jason, and when he returns acts another part. Gone is the defiant woman of earlier scenes; she is now humble, reasonable, submissive. To strengthen her plea for forgiveness she calls her sons and tells them to embrace their father. At this point, as she thinks of what must happen to them, her pretence slips and she is in danger of breaking down, but controls herself with an effort.

> My children, here, my children, leave the house.
> Come out to see your father, and with me
> Bid him good-bye. Be reconciled to friends
> And let your hatred die beside your mother's.
> We are at peace ; there is no anger now.
> Come, take his hand. Alas, the pity of it !
> There is something I cannot see, but my mind knows it.
> Children, will you live long to hold out
> Your loving arms as now ? My heart is heavy ;
> How close to tears I am, how full of fear.
> At last I have stopped the quarrel with their father
> And brought tears of forgiveness to their eyes.

Jason is completely won over, and delighted by the appeal to the children. He promises them a glorious future in Corinth, with kings to be their brothers. Medea takes the opportunity to press her request that the boys should take gifts to the princess and beg her to revoke their exile ; she herself is quite willing to leave the country. Jason demurs at first, but her arguments persuade him :

> They say that gifts can move the gods,
> A piece of gold is worth a thousand speeches.

So the children follow their father to the princess's home, taking with them the fatal gifts. A carping critic could object that there is another weakness in the play's structure here. There has been no point since Medea decided to use the poisoned robe when she could have left the stage to prepare it. But this is a fault of the tragic method rather than of Euripides. Scenes tend to be self-contained, and sometimes fail to cohere exactly with one another. There may often be loose ends in the plot development which a more naturalistic treatment would avoid.

The fate of the princess is sealed, and with it the fate of Medea's children. The chorus lament their inevitable deaths :

> There is no hope now for the children's lives,
> No hope any longer ; they go to their deaths,
> And the bride, poor bride, will accept the curse
> Of the golden crown,
> And with her own hands make death an ornament
> To set in her golden hair.
>
> The beauty and splendour and grace of the robe
> And the crown worked of gold will persuade her
>   to wear them.
> She will soon be dressed to marry the dead,
> Into such a trap will she fall,
> Into such deadly fate, poor lady, and never
> Escape from the curse upon her.

The Tutor hurries in to announce that the princess has accepted the gifts and pardoned the children. Medea turns away her head and bows it in grief. The children themselves return, and Medea bids them farewell in a scene among the most poignant in Greek drama, now weakening and embracing them, now forcing herself to

be resolute. The children's silence as their mother weeps
over them adds to the pathos.

> Ah, children, children, you have a city now
> And home, where when we've said our sad good-bye
> You will live out your lives without your mother.
> I go in exile to another land
> Before I have had the joy of seeing you happy.
> Before I make your marriage bed, and dress
> Your bride and carry torches at your wedding.
> My wilfulness has brought its own reward.
> For nothing did I toil to bring you up,
> For nothing did I labour and endure
> The pains I suffered in your hour of birth.
> Once I had, oh, once — such splendid hopes
> In you, to have you near me as I grew old,
> And when death came, your loving arms around me,
> What all men long for. That sweet dream is now
> Destroyed. When you and I have parted
> Your loving eyes will never look upon
> Your mother again ; you go to another life.
> My sons, my sons, why do you look at me ?
> Why smile at me, the last smile I shall see ?
> Oh, what shall I do ? Women, my heart
> Is faltering when I look at their bright eyes.
> I cannot do it. I renounce the plans
> I made before. My children shall come with me.
> Why should I use their suffering to hurt
> Their father, and so doubly hurt myself ?
> Not I, not I. I renounce my plans.
> And yet — what is the matter with me ? Shall I let
> My enemies go scot free and earn their scorn ?
> I must be bold. Why, what a coward am I
> That can allow my mind talk of relenting. . . .
> My children, give
> Your mother your hand, let mother hold your hand.
> O dearest hand, the lips I hold most dear.
> Dear face and dear proud eyes, bless you
> Wherever you may go ; your father leaves

You nothing here. O sweet embrace, the feel
Of your soft skin, the scent of children's breath
Go away, away. I have no strength to look
At you, my sorrows overwhelm me.
I know how evil is the thing I am to do.
But anger has proved stronger than our reason.
And from anger all our greatest ills arise.

The children enter the house. In them Euripides displays his consummate ability to turn apparent limitations to his own advantage. They are extra characters ; the three-actor rule means that they cannot speak, but Euripides uses their silent presence to paint the pathos of Medea's plight. Their silence is eloquent and haunting ; each time they appear we wonder if we are to see them again. Here they go off for the last time, pitiful, unprotesting figures caught up in the issues they cannot understand. A Messenger arrives, to announce that the princess is dead. His long speech is a fine example of Euripides' shock tactics. Her death is described in brutal, vivid detail. Nothing is omitted or glossed over. Behind the restraint of even the greatest Greek tragedy lurks a primitive savagery, the cruelty of the original myths. Though it was difficult to depict death on the stage, there was no limit to its description. Euripides piles on the horror until the mind reels beneath its impact.

Her colour goes, she stumbles sideways, back
Towards the throne, legs trembling, and just
Stops herself from falling on the floor.
Then some old waiting-maid, who must have thought
The fit was sent by Pan or by some god,
Began to pray : then saw her mouth all white
With running froth, her eyeballs starting from
Their sockets and blood gone from her face
And screamed so loud the screaming drowned

The prayer. . . .
From two directions the pain attacked her.
The golden circlet coiled around her hair
Poured forth strange fire, devouring everything.
And the fine-spun robe, the gift your children gave her,
Had teeth to tear the poor girl's pretty skin. . . .
Only her father would have recognized her.
Her eyes had lost their settled look, her face
Its natural appearance. From her head
Ran streams of blood to mingle with the fire.
Her flesh dropped from its bones like pine-tears, torn
By the unseen power of the devouring poison.
We saw, and shuddered ; no one dared to touch
The corpse, we had her fate for warning.
But her wretched father, not knowing what had happened
Came straight in, and flung himself on the body.
And as he knelt he wept, and put his arms
Around her, kissed her, talked to her — 'Poor daughter,
What god has killed you so inhumanly ?
Who takes you from me, from the grave of my
Old age ? If I could die with you, my child !'
And then he stopped his tears and lamentations
And tried to raise his old limbs up again,
But clung to the fine dress as ivy clings
To laurel branches. There was a ghastly struggle,
He wanting to get up off his knees and she
Holding him down. When he tried to push her off
He tore the ageing flesh from off his bones.
At last his strength gave out, the wretched man
Gave up the ghost, it was too much for him.

The Messenger ends his speech, as is customary in Euripides, with a moral reflection :

> I am not afraid to say, that those who seem
> Wise among men and accomplished talkers
> Must pay the heaviest penalty of all.
> No mortal man is happy. He might grow
> More prosperous, if fortune came his way,
> Than others, but happy he can never be.

Happy in the knowledge that her plot has succeeded, Medea steels herself for the last time to kill her children. She goes inside the house ; the chorus wait, breathless, for the result. As in *Agamemnon*, we hear the cries of the slain, made more poignant by the fact that this is the first time we have heard them speak. Jason enters, coming straight from the body of the princess to see to his children's safety. He is afraid that the King's kinsman will kill them in revenge. The chorus break the news that they are already dead. Jason is momentarily stunned by the news, then leaps to the door shouting for his men to unbar it. Here Euripides shows his mastery of dramatic situations. He deliberately uses a well-known formula ; commands to 'open the door' in such passages of tragedy are commonly preludes to the appearance of the *ekkyklema* with the bodies of the dead upon it. So the eyes of the audience are riveted on the central door, watching for it to open and reveal the customary tableau. Suddenly Medea's voice is heard ; by a brilliant stroke of surprise, a theatrical legerdemain, it comes not from the door but from above, over the roof. She rides in a chariot drawn by serpents, and clasps her children's bodies in her arms. This masterly tableau had a powerful effect on the audience. It is recorded for us by an ancient commentator, and was illustrated on several vase-paintings of the period and later. Jason demands his sons, she refuses. In curt, pungent verses they taunt each other with their own unhappiness. Euripides often connects his stories with the inauguration of some local rite. Here, Medea promises to create a solemn festival in Corinth to expiate the murder. Her magic chariot rumbles out of sight, leaving Jason to lament the deaths of his dearest and the chorus

to sum up the precariousness of human existence in a few
sad lines :

> Many things are ordered by Zeus in Olympus,
> And the gods do much beyond human imagining.
> The looked-for result fails to materialize
> While heaven finds ways to achieve the unexpected.
> So it has happened in this our story.

As a drama of moral issues the *Medea* does not invite comparison with *Agamemnon*. Its scope is narrower ; it deals
not with abstract ethical problems, but with more tangible
social questions — woman's status in a man's world, the
weakness of promises when opposed by self-interest. Yet
even to these problems Euripides does not pretend to give
an answer. Medea's supernatural powers beg the question.
At the beginning of the play she is Medea the abandoned
wife, at the end Medea the legendary sorceress. To
achieve an exciting conclusion social drama is abandoned
for fairy tale. The conclusion does not develop from the
plot, but is imposed on it from outside. It has been well
said that many an Athenian in the audience would have
seen his own problems reflected in the *Medea* but would
not have found them answered. Yet for all the moral
arguments in the world we would not forgo the sheer
theatrical excitement of those final scenes, the bitter
invective of the quarrels, or the acute perception of the
character-drawing. Even the smaller parts are vividly and
interestingly portrayed — the Nurse with her simple
loyalty ; the Tutor, malicious and full of below-stairs
gossip, with his affectation of worldly wisdom ; Creon,
uneasily conscious that he is in an indefensible moral
position, but using his family affection to justify it ; old
Aegeus, still recognizing obligations which the younger

generation had jettisoned. Euripides' characters are more human, and so psychologically more interesting. Only the Messenger was not so much a character as a piece of stage machinery.

The choruses too are better integrated with the play than is usual. So often with Euripides we feel that the chorus is there from convention rather than for any dramatic purpose, and that the dramatist would be happier without it. It is a commonplace of dramatic criticism that in Aeschylus the actors are gods and the chorus heroes, in Sophocles the actors heroes and the chorus mortals, in Euripides the actors mortal and the chorus mere shadows. In this play, apart from the difficulty we have noted, the chorus has something relevant to say and says it well. Their songs are beautifully composed in Euripides' finest manner. They represent ordinary people with ordinary emotions, torn between sympathy and horror. They typify Greek womanhood, patient un-questioning martyrs to the eternal tyranny of men. Even to-day the village women toil in the fields while their lords and masters drink and play draughts in the taverns. Against the background of their docility Medea's flouting of divine and human law stands out in sharp relief.

CHAPTER VII

SATYR PLAY: THE *CYCLOPS*

POLONIUS would have described the satyr play as tragical-comical-pastoral, and, if he truly represents the Elizabethan noble with his experience of courtly entertainments, would have felt more at home with it than we do. It comes nearer to the masque than anything we have to-day. Satyr play goes back to something more primitive than do either tragedy or comedy. It has the tragic form but few of its virtues. Played as an after-piece to a trilogy, it was intended as humorous relief, an antidote to the solemnity which preceded it. Tragedy had moral purpose, comedy was a medium of social comment, but satyr play was pure entertainment. The plays were amusing, light-hearted *divertissements* based on stories from popular mythology. It was an essential qualification that the chorus should be composed of satyrs, and, to judge from the examples we know, considerable liberties could be taken with the story to make this possible. A recurring figure was Silenus, father of the satyrs, a gross, drunken but kindly creature. Ancient critics gave Aeschylus first place in writing satyr play. Certainly the *Net-fishers*, fragments of which have been discovered in the sands of Egypt, seems superior to the longer pieces we possess. It opens with two characters looking out to sea. They spy a strange floating object, and wonder what it is.

'Is it a whale or a shark?' They try to drag it ashore in their nets, but it is too heavy. Here the fragment gives out, but they were probably assisted in the end by the satyr chorus. Their catch turns out to be a chest containing Danaë and the infant Perseus. A later scene, in unexpectedly tender mood, shows Silenus nursing and comforting the baby.

The *Searchers* of Sophocles, also fragmentary, tells how Apollo lost his cattle and the satyrs helped to look for them. They go through an elaborate pantomime of following the tracks, heads down, noses to ground. A sudden noise alarms them so much that they fall flat on their faces. They have never heard anything like it before. It is the first lyre, invented by the infant Hermes, who stole the cattle and led them backwards to reverse the tracks and baffle pursuit! The satyrs are shown as rough, boisterous creatures ready for anything so long as it is not dangerous, but terrified at once by the unexpected. Satyr plays are full of animal spirits and earthy humour.

The *Cyclops* of Euripides, the only satyr play to be preserved complete, takes for plot the well-known adventures of Odysseus in Sicily, described in Book Eleven of the *Odyssey*. Silenus, shaggy and pot-bellied, with a red, shining bald pate, advances on to the stage brandishing an iron rake to deliver the prologue. Pointing to the *skene* door, he tells us that it is the cave of the Cyclops, Polyphemus. He explains how he and the satyrs come to be there — needless to say, they are not present in the Homeric version. The prologue is well written and has an unexpected pathos when he laments his lost comforts and sighs nostalgically for their old life. Half reproachfully he invokes his old master Bacchus.

From boyhood, Bacchus, when my blood was hot,
My whole life long have I laboured in your service
And paid for my passion with a thousand pains.
There was first Hera's fury, that forced you to fly
Away from the mountains and the nymphs that nursed you ;
Then the fight we fought with our foes the giants
When I stood by your shoulder, spear in hand,
And struck Enceladon's shield a crack
That dropped him dead — what's that ? I dreamt it ?
Why, Bacchus, I brought my booty to show you !
But the past was child's play to our present plight.
There were some Tuscans, pirates by trade,
Whom Hera aroused and put it in their heads
To carry you off to the ends of the earth.
When they brought me the news I embarked with my boys
In pursuit of the pirates — I perched in the prow
To steer the ship straight, while my sons at the oars
Sat sweating and straining, and stirred the grey sea
To foam with their flailing, as we followed you, Lord.
But when our course carried us close off Malea
Came a keen East wind that encompassed our ship
And cast up the crew on the cliffs of Etna.
Here the sea-god's sons, the one-eyed Cyclopes,
Haunt hollow caves ; human flesh is their food.
One such creature caught us and kept us for slaves
Immured in his cavern. Men call our master,
This fiend, Polyphemus. Our feasting forgotten,
We serve this Cyclops and shepherd his flocks.
My sons spend their days on the spur of the hill,
My young with his, his ewes and his lambs,
While I stay inside, to clean out the cave,
Fill troughs for the flock, and furnish the board
With the monstrous meals that my master requires.

As he finishes speaking there is a burst of music off stage.
The satyrs bound on, leaping and dancing, going through
the motions of herding their flocks. Animals are notoriously difficult to handle in the theatre, and no producer

in his right mind would allow a flock of sheep on the stage. Here they only exist in the audience's imagination, and the action of herding is conveyed by dance and mime. Greek dramatic dances were highly expressive. They sing a jolly rustic song :

> Billy boy, where are you biding ?
>   Come from the mountain-side, come.
> Up among the hill-tops hiding,
>   Come from the mountain-side, come.
> Shelter here from bitter weather,
> Wind and storm will harm you never.

But Silenus' attention has been attracted by something off stage.

> I see a Greek ship come ashore close by
> And the master mariners, commander and all,
> Coming to the cave with casks on their shoulders
> To fill with fresh water, and forage for food
> In the baskets they bear.

The stranger is Odysseus, who enters with a number of his men. Silenus knows him by reputation, and cross-questions him. Odysseus demands in turn where they are. When he learns whose cave it is, he is alarmed, but Silenus assures him that the Cyclops is out hunting. Odysseus asks for food. All Silenus has to offer is the Cyclops' sheep, but is prepared to bargain. What scruples he has are overcome by a present of wine. It is years since he last tasted it. He raises the skin to his mouth, drinks ecstatically and dances with delight. As the sailors are about to leave with lambs and cheese from the Cyclops' store, the monster is heard returning. Silenus loses his Dutch courage and runs in panic into the cave, but

Odysseus resolves to face this new danger as he has faced
many others.

> Shall I fly one foe, and surrender the fame
> Of my triumphs at Troy ? Why, time and again
> I stood under shield against Trojans a score.
> If death is our due, we will die without shame.
> And if we live still, let our fame live longer.

The Cyclops enters, a grotesque figure ; his mask has one
large eye in the middle of his forehead, and he is dressed
in shaggy skins. He bellows at the satyrs, accusing them
of idleness and demanding his meal. It does not take him
long to discover the sailors, with his lambs trussed up to
be taken away. It is only too clear what has been going on,
and his anger knows no bounds. Silenus has occupied the
interval in providing himself with an excuse. He comes
in with his hands clasped to his bald head, moaning and
groaning and pretending that he has been assaulted.

Odysseus indignantly denies that he took the sheep by
force. A desperate argument follows as Silenus, Odysseus
and the chorus accuse each other. The Cyclops will listen
to no excuses. This is an excellent opportunity to vary
his diet by eating the sailors for supper. Odysseus makes
a vain attempt to appeal to his finer feelings. He invokes
the Cyclops' father, Poseidon, whose temples they had
protected from invaders in the Trojan War.

> We beseech you, great son of the sea-god your sire,
> And pray for your pardon in good plain words.
> To kill us and cook us would be a crime,
> For we are the warriors, worthiest lord,
> Who fought for your father and helped to uphold
> His shrines in safe keeping on Hellas' far shores. . . .
> It is law among men, and custom demands it,
> That castaways craving for kindness and shelter
> Should depart dry-apparelled with presents in their packs,

Not to be skewered on spits, like swine from the sty,
Or give their bodies to glut your greed.
We have lost enough lives in the land of Priam,
That, bloated with blood and the bodies of the slain,
Made widows of wives, made mothers weep,
Stole sons from grey sires ; should we who survived
Be flung in the fire to fill your foul feast,
Where may a man turn ? Be admonished by me.
Repress your proud stomach, repent of your sins.
Give ear to good counsel ; our gains full often
Are levelled to loss when unlawfully won.

The Cyclops replies in a barbarous, cynical speech. He
cares nothing for the gods, only for his own pleasures.

The wise have but one god, wealth, little man.
All others are air, and empty talk.
For the shrines by my sire on the sea-shore founded,
Destroy them, I care not — why tell me of these ?
I take no thought for Zeus's thunders
Nor grant him a greater god than I.
I care not what comes, and will show you the cause,
If you mark my words well : when he wills it to rain
I have a dry dwelling indoors in my cave
Where I feast on roast flesh or on wild-fowl
And gulp down my gullet a gallon of milk.
So I sprawl on my back, my stomach skywards,
And it rumbles deriding the thunder's roar.
When wild winds from Thrace bring winter snow,
I bind my body in beast-skins warm,
Set flame to my fire, and frost cannot harm me.
The earth each year, if it wishes or no,
Must furnish fresh pasture to fatten my flocks.
I sacrifice sheep to no man but myself
And to none of the gods but my belly, the greatest.
The worldly wise have one god alone.
To dine and drink deep every livelong day
And let the world pass. These men who make laws
To trouble and tease us and take up our time,
I scorn all such, and shall ever pursue

My soul's satisfaction by swallowing you!
You shall have gifts, I am not ungracious —
A cauldron to cook you, a fire beneath,
My sire's sea-water to stew your bones.
Now step inside, and stand at the altar.
A sight for sore stomachs, to gladden my god!

With this he drives Odysseus and his men inside ; the doors close. To ill-treat a stranger requesting hospitality was to the Greek mind one of the greatest of crimes. The satyrs, subdued and apprehensive, reflect on this in a long chorus which paints the horror of the situation in no uncertain terms. Then another door opens and Odysseus, in an attitude of horror, slips outside. He has discovered another way out, though he does not mean to desert his men. He tells the satyrs what has happened inside.

When we came to the cave in the cliff so deep
He kindled a fire, then flung on the flames
The helm of an oak, so huge and heavy
I wonder three wagons could carry the weight.
Then strewed a soft couch for himself at the hearthside,
A pile of thick pine-needles plucked from the bough. . . .
When all was arranged in order, he took,
This hell-cook, god-hated, in one huge swing
Two men from among us and unmade them both,
One struck on the stewpot till the bronze resounded,
One held by the heel, and hammered his head
On a sharp spur of rock till his brains spilled out,
Seized knife, sliced him, set some to roast
And put some apart in a pot to boil.
I wept as I watched what they underwent
And tiptoed towards them to await my turn.
My friends, in fear, like a flock of poor birds,
Crept into corners, their colour all gone.

Then, Odysseus says, he had a marvellous inspiration. He persuaded the Cyclops to drink the wine which had already

tempted Silenus. The monster was delighted with this
new pleasure, and drank so heartily that he began to sing.
He was rapidly falling into a drunken stupor. While he
is asleep Odysseus plans to blind him by boring out his
solitary eye with a red-hot stake. He asks the satyrs to
help. They agree willingly — they are more than anxious
to escape from the island. Inside the *skene* the Cyclops'
roaring grows louder. As the satyrs dance and sing a
merry drinking song, the doors burst open and he reels
out to join them, followed by Silenus with the wine-skin.

CHORUS. Our drinking songs are merry things
With friends to join the chorus.
Wine will give your spirit wings.
Such joys the grape holds for us.

CYCLOPS. Oho, so full of wine am I,
And heavy with much drinking,
Like a ship that's loaded high
And precious near to sinking.

A glorious night to sing and shout
And dance among the clover,
Brothers, come and help me out,
Friends, pass the wine-skin over.

The Cyclops, in a fit of drunken amiability, is anxious to
share this new delight with his brothers on the island.
Odysseus persuades him that it is too good to give away,
while Silenus takes advantage of their distracted attention
to take a drink or two on the sly. 'What will you give
me', Odysseus asks, 'in return for the wine?' The
Cyclops retorts that he will show his gratitude by not
eating Odysseus — until he has eaten all the others first.
Picking up Silenus, he carries him kicking and struggling
inside the cave. Odysseus pauses to give the satyrs a last

word of encouragement, and to pray to Hephaestus, the
Fire-God, before following him.

> Hephaestus, thou that feedest Etna's fires,
> Burn out the bright eye of this beast thy neighbour
> And rid this realm of thy rival for ever.
> And Sleep, sweet nurseling of sombre Night,
> Bring thy power to bear on this godless brute
> Lest Odysseus be undone, and the mighty deeds
> He wrought in the Trojan War be wasted
> By a monster unmindful of god or man.
> Else must we agree that chance is our god,
> The greatest of gods, that governs all others.

The chorus, left alone, sing with bloodthirsty relish of
their coming revenge. It soon appears that singing is all
they intend to do, for when Odysseus comes out to urge
them on they all find excuses. Nervously they back away
from the door ; one has sprained his ankle, another is too
far away, a third has dust in his eyes and cannot see.
Odysseus is disgusted at their cowardice, and sees that he
and his sailors must manage by themselves. The satyrs
are quite ready to contribute another song :

> So shall we do, gallant Ithacan stranger,
> Sing you a song as the stake spins about.
> Ours is the cheering and yours is the danger,
> See if our shanty will tumble it out!
> Heave ho, my hearties, heave faster and stronger,
> Singe his great eyebrows and make the beast roar!
> Blind him and burn him and let him no longer
> Shepherd his sheep on our mountainous shore!

The beast roars indeed ; a piercing scream echoes from
inside the cave and the blinded Cyclops staggers out — the
blindness is shown by a change of mask — howling abuse
at the sailors who have tricked him. The satyrs take a
fiendish delight in taunting him, skipping nimbly out of

his way as he crawls round trying to find his persecutors. Misdirected by the chorus he throws himself from one side of the stage to the other, but Odysseus and his men slip out easily. At last the Cyclops bangs his head and crouches stunned. For the first time Odysseus reveals his real name, and the Cyclops is horrified.

CYCLOPS. Why, what did you say ? What name is this ?
ODYSSEUS. My name is Odysseus — so my father called me.
 Did you think to insult me and escape scot free ?
 Much good it did us to drag Troy down
 If you feasted on my friends, and I forgave you.
CYCLOPS. As the prophets foretold, it has come to pass,
 That I should be blinded by you and your band
 In your travels from Troy. This too they foretold,
 That to pay for my pain you should pine long years
 Adrift on the deep ere your journey is done.
ODYSSEUS. Go perish, I pray you, the prophecy's complete.
 Come friends, to the coast, and cast off our keel
 To Sicily's sea and my ancestral home.
CYCLOPS. No, rogue, for I'll wrench this rock from its seat
 And cast it to crush you, crew and all.
 This cliff I'll climb, though I cannot see ;
 One way or another my foot shall find !

His threats do not trouble Odysseus. He and the satyrs go off in happy procession singing a short triumphant chorus :

 We'll sail with King Odysseus
 To Etna's lonely shore,
 To find our old Lord Bacchus
 And serve him evermore.

The main obstacle to our appreciation of this play is its brutal theme. The transitions from jovial good humour to horror are too frequent and abrupt for modern taste. Euripides takes an unashamed delight in bloodthirsty details. Odysseus' long description of the death of his friends and the relish with which the satyrs dwell on the Cyclops' punishment are too frank for to-day's audiences, though the Greeks with their broader outlook found nothing displeasing. A primitive cruelty pervades the play, which did not offend the Greeks but disturbs us. For all his crimes and however well his punishment is deserved, it is not pleasant to see the Cyclops crawling round the stage like a wounded animal, taunted by Odysseus and the satyrs. Euripides loved powerful effects of this nature. In the tragedies the full horror is masked to some extent by the beauty of his language, but in this short and slight piece it is seen to its full effect, and we are correspondingly repelled.

In many ways the *Cyclops* is an unsatisfactory play. Apart from its brutal theme, it gives the impression of having been written in a great hurry. This is seen particularly in the choruses. Though the first is of normal length, the rest grow shorter and shorter throughout the play, as though there had not been time to write more. Much of the character-drawing derives directly from Homer. The one original character, Silenus, is amusingly portrayed ; he is greedy, cunning, deceitful, brave until put to the test, ready to do anything for a sip of wine. For all this he remains lovable, and his speeches have occasional unexpected touches of pathos. He is a Falstaffian figure, refined in some degree from the gross and obscene Sileni of vase paintings.

The Cyclops is monster, nothing more. Many of the touches of so-called Euripidean philosophy which scholars have found in him — his atheism, for example — are in fact pure Homer. Though sometimes comic, as in the drinking chorus, he remains at best a bogy-man. Odysseus himself has little individuality. There seems to be some attempt at the beginning of the play to parody the pride of the military hero, but that is all.

In one respect the *Cyclops* has great interest for students of the Greek theatre. As we are able to read the Homeric story and the play side by side we have a good example of the technique of adaptation for the stage, and can see how far the dramatist had to remodel and amplify his sources. The alterations in the *Cyclops* show clearly under what limitations the theatre worked. First and most important, the action in Homer takes place almost entirely inside the cave — Odysseus and his men enter it when they arrive, and the Cyclops finds them there on his return. As the theatre could not show interiors, all the important action had to be moved outside. This leads to some improbabilities. Odysseus, for example, has to slip out 'through a rift in the rock' to narrate what has happened to his men. He tells us that he is too honourable to escape himself and leave the others behind.

> I'll not seek safety by deserting my friends,
> Though escape I could, for I quit the cave
> Through a rift in the rock, and the rest are inside.
> Shall I alone live, and relinquish the men
> In whose company I came ? It would be a crime.

This excuse only makes the inconsistency more obvious. If coming and going were so easy for Odysseus, why could not his friends follow him ? Transferring the action to outside has one advantage ; the blinding of the Cyclops can reasonably take place out of the audience's sight.

One other scenic point is worth attention. In Homer the Cyclops bars the cave with a huge stone on leaving.

There is no mention of this in Euripides, another indication that the play did not use representational scenery. If it had, it would have been easy to reproduce the incident with the stone ; its absence is significant. In Homer, too, the Cyclops is a giant. This was impossible in the theatre, so Euripides is careful to avoid any reference to super-human stature.

The most important difference comes at the end of the play, when Odysseus and his men escape from the cave. In Homer the blinded Cyclops sits at the entrance to catch them as they emerge, but they cheat him by hanging underneath his sheep ; the Cyclops runs his hands along the sheep's backs, and does not suspect that anything is amiss. This incident is delightfully parodied in the *Wasps* of Aristophanes, when an old father imprisoned at home by his son tries to escape by tying himself underneath a donkey. As we have seen, it would have been impracticable to have a flock of sheep on the stage, so Euripides falls back on the weak alternative of making the men slip out as Polyphemus runs from one side to the other.

Neat though the adaptation is, it leaves several loose ends, particularly in the time-sequence. In Homer the action is spread over several days, in Euripides it must be presented as a series of consecutive incidents with no long gaps. But the dramatist has tacked together the essential episodes from Homer without seeing that they cohere accurately. The satyrs' entrance with their flocks presumably sets the time as evening : the Cyclops enters demanding his breakfast, and immediately afterwards the chorus speak of the stars they can see in the sky, bringing us back to night again without even an intervening chorus to mark the passage of time.

Thus many points indicate haste in the composition of this play. This is understandable — the output of the tragic poets was prodigious. One has a picture of the harassed playwright who had devoted too long to writing the required three tragedies, finding himself with barely time to complete the satyr play to go with them, and sitting down in haste to adapt something from Homer that would suit his purpose. Though the *Cyclops* is not a great play, it shows the Greek theatre as a place not solely devoted to the leisured contemplation of masterpieces, but one where, as to-day, work had to be completed to time and was sometimes rushed in the execution. An inferior play may teach us more about the theatre than a great one. The *Cyclops*, lacking Euripides' usual polish, makes it easier to inspect the workings of his invention.

CHAPTER VIII

COMEDY: ARISTOPHANES
AND THE *BIRDS*

B Y an accident of history, Greek comedy and Aristophanes are almost synonymous. Eleven of his plays are the only complete examples to come down to us. His predecessors and contemporaries are represented by a large body of fragments of varying length and tributes to their powers in other authors, his successors by two near-complete plays of Menander, more fragments, and what can be deduced of the Greek plays from their Roman imitations. If the work of a whole period is to be represented by one man, we could hardly have a better. Aristophanes was not consistently successful ; some of his work was caviare to the general, and he won only four first prizes, three second and one third. But there is no doubt that he was the cleverest poet of his time. His life, too, covers the radical change in the Greek theatre when Athens' defeat by Sparta made free speech dangerous. There is a marked transition from the uninhibited licence of his first plays to the innocuous allegory of his last.

His busy pen was ready to treat any subject that offered material for humour. Attempts have been made to tie him down to one particular creed or political party. His attacks on new projects and ideas have been cited as evidence for his conservatism, but it is dangerous to carry this argument too far. A comic playwright must have something to be funny about. Novelties, speculations, innovations, anything that is in the public eye, are legitimate targets for his humour. Nevertheless he could still hit out at the great figures of the past when inclined. On the other hand, there is no doubt that he seriously disapproved of the new type of politician — *nouveaux riches*, tradesmen whose loud voices and popular appeal were now shaping Athenian policy for the worse.

One of his earliest plays, the *Babylonians*, was a violent attack on the demagogue Cleon. For this he was impeached and fined (the charge was that he had ridiculed a leader of the state in front of visiting officials and ambassadors). Nothing daunted, he attacked Cleon again in the *Knights*. Demos, the People, is represented as an old man guided in everything by his steward, a caricature of Cleon. Two slaves, thinly disguised portraits of prominent generals, unseat him by setting up in opposition someone even more vulgar and self-opinionated, a sausage-seller. After a lengthy debate the sausage-seller carries the day.

For the greater part of Aristophanes' life men's thoughts were concerned with the war, and three of his plays take it as their subject. The *Acharnians*, produced in 425 when the war had been going on for six years, shows an elderly Athenian, tired of restrictions and the waste of public money in useless diplomacy, who decides to negotiate a separate peace with the enemy on his own behalf, and open up a free market of his own. This meets with great success. An informer (in a modern play he would be a Ministry official) who comes spying is sold to a customer as a typical Athenian product. The play closes with a contrast between the joys of peace and the hardships of war. On one side of the stage the old man prepares a banquet; on the other a general buckles on his armour to go off and fight. In the *Peace* (421) another Athenian ascends to heaven to drag Peace out of a well into which War has thrown her. The *Lysistrata*, a later play, tells how the women of Greece secured peace for their cities by refusing to associate with their husbands till they stop fighting.

Aristophanes' third favourite theme is one of which comic poets never tired, the parody of fashionable intellectual movements of the day. We have already mentioned the *Clouds*, a broad burlesque of Socrates and his school. Euripides is a frequent butt. Aristophanes was fascinated by his cleverness and wit. His tragedies had a theatrical brilliance and gift for perverse argument that the comic poet appreciated ; this is obvious from the way in which he quotes them. But all the conservative in Aristophanes rose up against the destructive philosophy for which Euripides stood and he loses no opportunity of ridiculing him on the stage. In the *Frogs* his songs, prologues and characterization are mercilessly pulled to pieces. In the *Thesmophoriazusae* he appears again. He has heard that the women of Athens are after his blood for attacking women in his plays, and disguises his relative Mnesilochus as a woman to spy on them at their festival. Mnesilochus attempts to defend the poet, but is inevitably discovered and held prisoner. There follows a sustained burlesque of tragic scenes and conventions. Euripides enters disguised as various characters from his plays, and he and Mnesilochus act scenes from them in an attempt to baffle the stupid sentry and escape. These parodies are invaluable material for the theatrical historian.

With the fall of Athens his work changed. The democracy was soon restored, but not its old freedom. Criticism of the régime, even free philosophical thought, was dangerous. So Aristophanes confined himself to topics unlikely to give offence. *Women in Parliament* (391) shows women disguising themselves as men to take over the government and establish a communist state. It may be in part a parody of current communistic ideals such as those of Plato's *Republic*. *Wealth* (388) is a straight-forward allegory. The blind God of Wealth has his sight restored, and begins to bestow riches on the deserving, not haphazardly as before, much to the dismay of certain classes of the population. These non-personal, non-political plays, though amusing enough, lack the force of his earlier work ; his genius suffered under restraint. When the comic chorus was forbidden to express itself freely there was no reason for its existence, and so it gradually disappears. In style, these last two plays point the way to the New Comedy of Menander. They are impersonal, inoffensive, pleasing without stimulating. In-offensive, one must add, only in a political sense ; the *Women in Parliament* remains highly obscene.

The description of the style of Greek comedy in Chapter II is necessarily a description of Aristophanes, and there is no need to repeat it here. It must be emphasized that his greatest quality, and his most distinctive, was the versatility which enabled him to jump from one extreme to the other without sacrificing either dramatic continuity or audience interest. His plots are a series of sketches built round a central character and theme. It has been objected that he created no great comic character, like Shakespeare's Falstaff, but we should not expect him to.

The conditions of his art forbade it. Greek comedy was comedy of situation, not of character. Perhaps he comes nearest to it in the elderly Athenians who are the protagonists in many plays, shrewd, cunning, persuasive, with a keen eye for the main chance.

In his language Aristophanes allows himself great freedom. The talk of his characters, succinct and punctuated with oaths, reflects the conversation of the man in the street. He revels in puns and elaborate word-play, nor is he afraid to invent new words or fanciful compounds when necessary. Several of his characters speak in broad dialect, and he pokes fun at the unintelligible gibberish of foreigners trying to speak Greek. Thus Aristophanes' language is not the artificial language of tragedy but the everyday talk of street, tavern and market-place. Against this we must set the elegance and beauty of his choral lyrics. Both qualities are strongly marked in the play we are to consider.

THE *BIRDS*

We have already seen how the topicality of Aristophanes' work makes it difficult to appreciate to-day. We cannot fully understand the *Knights* unless we know who Cleon was, and what he stood for. Much of the satire of the *Clouds* is lost to us unless we are familiar with the outlines of sophistic philosophy and the contemporary attitude to it. True, study helps, but the humour tends to evaporate in the frequent journeys between text and glossary. Aristophanes wrote for the stage, and the schoolroom has always been unsympathetic to his genius. To explain a joke is the surest way of killing it.

The humour of the *Birds*, however, is eternal and universal. Though containing many topicalities, it is a romantic extravaganza as easily appreciated to-day as when it was first written. Aristophanes wrote it in 414, when after many fluctuations the war at last seemed to be taking a turn for the better. There were high hopes that the great expedition to Sicily would restore the city's fallen fortunes. Much of the bitterness of the past was forgotten. The Athenians, always volatile, were in a mood of happy expectancy. This sense of well-being is present throughout the *Birds*. Attempts have been made to prove the play a detailed allegory of the Sicilian situation, every joke having a reference to current politics, but these arguments are laborious and often contradictory. It is a favourite academic game to discover meanings that the author never intended. The *Birds* is pure fantasy; if it reflects the political situation at all, it does so only in its mood. Although by now experienced in the practical side of the theatre, the author entrusted its production to someone else. Surprisingly, it won only second prize.

Comedy demands more realism than tragedy. As it was impossible to 'discover' characters on the Greek stage, a common device to open the play was to bring on characters as if they had just reached the end of a journey. This is what happens here. Two old Athenians hobble in, footsore and weary, carrying a heap of luggage. They complain volubly of the distance they have covered. One carries a crow, the other a jackdaw, intended to act as guides to their destination. They are looking for the Kingdom of the Birds, ruled by Tereus the Hoopoe, a mythical character who was once a human being but was changed into a bird for his sins. The birds are poor guides. For the moment the steps from stage to orchestra represent a rocky path ; the two men wander haphazardly up and down, trying to make sense out of the birds' directions. At last one of them stops, gazes round the ranks of spectators and addresses them despairingly.

> Isn't it tragic we should come up here
> And wanting nothing but to get the bird,
> Then be unable to find out the way ?
> For we, good audience, are sick with a disease
> Quite opposite to that which Sacas had,
> A displaced person, whom no state would take
> Until at last he elbowed into ours.
> But we're of honest birth and good connections
> As good as the next man ; we weren't shooed off
> But flew away from Athens — on our feet.
> Not that we hate the city that we've left.
> Not that it isn't great and heaven-blessed
> And quite impartial in collecting fines.
> The cicadas sit on the branches singing
> A month or two ; but the men of Athens
> Spend lung power in law courts all their lives.
> That's why we've packed our holy jug and basket
> And myrtle wreaths, and started on our journey.
> We're looking round for some untroubled place
> Where we can settle down and rusticate.
> This expedition is in search of Tereus
> The hoopoe, wanting information from him
> If he's had a bird's-eye view of some such place.

The 'holy jug and basket' and myrtle wreath are among the luggage they carry on their backs ; they are to be used in offering sacrifice when they find somewhere they would like to stay. This was the regular procedure when a new colony was founded. The Athenians' love of litigation was often satirized. Aristophanes wrote a whole comedy, the *Wasps*, about it.

At last the birds seem to have made up their minds. They lead their owners up the steps for the last time. The men shout and stamp their feet, and suddenly a bird appears. He is so fantastically dressed that they fall down in fright. We have some idea of his costume from a fifth-century vase painting of a chorus dressed as birds. It dates from before the production of this play, and so cannot be an illustration of it, but the costumes used here would be similar. The dancers wear close-fitting tunics and tights stuck with feathers, and wear beaked half-masks. The beak of the bird in this play is so large that the Athenians make sarcastic comments about it. After some badinage they persuade him to go and fetch the king. He protests that Tereus is 'fast asleep, after his gnat and myrtle berry dinner', but eventually goes.

Comic actors had to work hard. In the *Birds* an unusually large number of characters appear in rapid succession. The actor playing the Bird has to go straight off to change his mask and reappear almost at once as Tereus. While he is gone the Athenians accuse each other of cowardice — both had lost their birds when they fell down. Tereus enters with a flourish, and takes up a tragic attitude. His divine punishment was a well-known tragic theme, and Aristophanes points this by putting into his mouth bombastic, high-flown phrases, a parody of tragic speech. His mask is grotesque ; it has lost most of its feathers, a fact which the travellers are not slow to comment upon. Altogether he is a ridiculous object. They explain the purpose of their visit, to find 'some well-padded spot, a feather-bed place snug to settle down'. Tereus makes several suggestions, none of which find favour but which give opportunity for jokes about personalities in the audience. This is the sort of humour that must inevitably pass us by, but it is worth quoting as an example of the sort of thing the Athenians enjoyed.

TEREUS. I see, you want an aristocracy!
EUELPIDES.   Not I!
    I can't abide the sight of Scellias' son.
    (*Scellias' son was called Aristocrates.*)
TEREUS. There's a flourishing city of the sort you mention
    On the Red Sea coast.
EUELPIDES.   No, that won't do.
    We'd never like the coast, where every dawn
    Might bring a boat with extradition papers.
TEREUS. Well, why not go to Eleia to live,
    In Lepreos?
EUELPIDES.   No, I haven't seen it.
    But I've seen Melanthius! Leprous! Not for me!
TEREUS. And what of the Opuntians in Locris?
    A charming neighbourhood.
EUELPIDES.   No place for me,
    I wouldn't be Opuntius for a fortune.

The puns may seem laboured now, but they were gloriously topical then. Unfortunately, jokes die with their subjects ; that is the tragedy of comedy.

    The Athenians ask about life among the birds. Finding that it needs no money, they are immediately attracted. One of them has been quiet for some time, wrapped in thought. He suddenly leaps up and shouts with glee. He has had a marvellous inspiration. Why not build a city for the birds ? They already have a strong strategic position.

    Air lies between Earth and Heaven.
Just as Athenians who want to visit Pytho
Must get a transit visa through Boeotia,
So when mankind makes offerings to heaven
You'll stop the smoke ascending to the gods
Unless they pay a toll-tax to the birds !

Without the smell of the sacrifices the gods will starve to
death. Tereus is thrilled with the plan, and runs off to
wake his wife, the Nightingale. They will summon the
other birds together. He leaves the stage so that the songs
which follow may be sung by a trained singer. The voice
of the Nightingale which eventually accompanies him is
represented by a flute. With a sudden change of mood
typical of comedy, the two songs now put into Tereus'
mouth are of real beauty. The first appeals to his wife
to sing, in the memory of their dead son Itys ; the second
summons the birds of every kind to come for a conference.

> Shed thy slumbers, mistress mine,
> And sound the sacred song
> With broken heart and voice divine
> For Itys, my dear son and thine,
> For whom we wept so long.
> Trilling from your tawny throat
> The sound through groves untrod
> Will pass, and every blessed note,
> Clear as a temple bell, will float
> Up to the throne of God.
> Apollo, with his ivory lyre,
> Will catch thy voice ere long,
> And with accompaniment inspire
> The gods to dance ; and heaven's choir
> Will harmonize your song.

Birds of a feather, come here to me now !
Birds from the teeming fields of the country
Feeding on barley and farmers' sowings,
Swift-winged, sweet-voiced, come in your thousands.
Birds that gather to follow the ploughshare,
Twittering over the upturned furrows.
Golden-voiced birds, leave your homes and come.

Woodland birds building nests in the ivy,
Abandon your leafy kingdom and come.

Birds of the hills plucking berries from branches
Of olive and arbute, fly to my call.
Birds catching gnats in the olive-green gorges,
Marsh-birds haunting the meadows of Marathon,
Flame-coloured bird, come kingfisher, come!
Sea-birds skimming the swell of the ocean,
Halcyon's mates in the trough of the wave,
Come to hear what we have to say!
We summon our clan to a great assembly,
All the tribe of the long-necked birds ;
Two shrewd old men have come to visit us,
Full of invention and highly original —
Come every one of you, come to the conference!
Come, come, come, come!

The chorus, colourfully and fantastically dressed, enters
the orchestra, not in the stately procession of a tragic
chorus, but in ones and twos, running wildly round,
fluttering and gesticulating. Each is made up as a different
kind of bird. There is an owl, a cock, a jay, a starling, a
lark, a hawk, a cuckoo and others besides. Tereus intro-
duces them one by one, with more jokes at the expense
of the audience, some of whom are compared with birds
to their discredit.

The chorus is far from docile. As soon as they hear
that two men are in their midst they grow fierce and
advance on them in a threatening manner. Tereus holds
them off and persuades them to listen. So the Athenian —
we learn later that his name is Pisthetairus, 'Persuasive'
— embarks on a long speech to convince the birds that
they were the first-born of creation and so the true rulers
of mankind. It is a mock history of the origin of the
world, full of comic examples to show how superior
birds are to the gods. First came the wren ; she came into
being before even the earth, and so when her father died

had nowhere to bury him ! The cuckoo tells men when it is harvest-time ; the cock tells us to wake in the mornings. Kings carry images of birds on their sceptres — even gods take birds for their symbols.

Permit me to call the best witness of all, great Zeus the omnipotent king,
Who bears on his brow a great eagle even now as ostensible proof of the thing,
And Athena an owl, that omniscient fowl, and Apollo the healer, a hawk.

This great heritage has been lost ; the birds are now mankind's slaves.

They treat you like madmen from bedlam,
Throw stones at your head if you let them,
Bring lime to your lairs,
Wires, cages and snares,
And come to the temples to set them.
They feel if you have any eggs,
And hang you in clumps by the legs.
It adds to your shame
You're not even fair game
But disposed of like offal and dregs.
They won't serve you roast, if you please,
But with hot olive oil and with cheese,
And silphium of course,
To make a fine sauce,
And cover your carcase with these.

He tells them how to recover their old empire by building a wall between Earth and Heaven and starving the gods into submission.

When once it is finished your trouble's diminished ; demand the royal sceptre from Zeus,
And if he says 'No', and won't let it go, and is strongly inclined to refuse,

Declare holy war, and lock up your door ; the gods will soon
   change their demeanours
When they're locked up above and deprived of the love of
   their Semeles and their Alcmenas.

As for mankind, the birds can subdue them by eating their
crops, and if they accept the new rule, give them all sorts
of blessings — they can give weather reports to the sailors,
discover mines and treasure-trove and, as birds live so
much longer than men, even give them extra years of
life !

This nonsense-speech is in the best Aristophanic vein.
It wins the birds over completely. The two men go off
with the Hoopoe to be fitted with wings, and the chorus
is left alone to sing with the Nightingale, her voice again
represented by a flute. They turn to face the audience.
The long chorus that follows is composed of several
elements ; first, another burlesque account of the birds'
part in creation ; then the *pnigos*, a familiar feature of the
comic chorus. This is a short piece designed to be spoken
by the chorus leader in one breath. Gilbert and Sullivan's
patter-songs are a good modern equivalent.

> If you greet with acclamation
> Our divine self-ordination,
> We are free for consultation
> On prophetic divination
> And the seasons' circulation
> And the art of orchestration.
> Not like Zeus abuse our station
> Hid in lofty isolation
> In the nearest cloud-formation,
> But bestow our presentations
> On successive generations
> Of our milk for your potations,
> Comic plays and recitations

> And a healthy expectation
> Of long life with your relations,
> And your blessing-loaded nation
> Bring to wealthy elevation.

They also sing a description of the virtues of wings, and the chorus contains occasional lyric verses of great beauty.

> So the swans are used to sing,
> Watching close by Hebron's banks,
> Marking time with beat of wing
> Their hymn of thanks.

> Ocean slumbers, breezes die.
> Forest beasts allay their fears.
> Throned upon a tranquil sky,
> Apollo hears.

> Wonder seizes heaven's lords,
> Fills Olympus with amaze,
> Muses, Graces, strike the chords
> Of hymns of praise.

The audience is offered all manner of inducements to become birds.

> If your customs debar you from striking papa, with the birds
> it's a positive virtue.
> Slap his face, say 'Old cock, to your spurs you must look. I
> regret that I'm going to hurt you'.

Runaway slaves, traitors, everyone who finds life on earth uncongenial is welcome to immigrate to birdland and enjoy the new freedom.

As the chorus ends Euelpides and Pisthetairus run on, laughing and joking, with wings on their shoulders. With Tereus they decide on a name for their new city — 'Cloudcuckooland' — and go on to sacrifice to the gods. Nowhere is the freedom of comedy more obvious than in its treatment of religion. What would happen to a modern dramatist who parodied Church ritual on the stage ? The nearest we have come to it in this country is in the mediaeval Feast of Misrule led by a mock Bishop or other religious dignitary, and this was soon suppressed by the Church. In three plays Aristophanes parodies the ritual of the sacrifice, though the moment of sacrifice itself is never reached — the proceedings are interrupted, or some excuse is made. It was probably felt that this would be going too far, even in the spirit of comedy. Towards the end of the play the gods themselves are introduced and made fun of. Serious and comic elements alternated in the mediaeval mystery plays — Noah turns from talking with God to argue with a nagging wife, and a knockabout comedy scene in which a sheep is disguised as a baby is followed by one of deep religious feeling in which the same shepherds present their gifts to the Child Jesus — yet even these have nothing comparable to the licence of Greek comedy. The spirit of topsy-turvydom in which comedy was born does not allow even the gods to escape scot-free. Dionysus himself, whose festival it was and whose priest was the chief spectator, is the leading character of the *Frogs* ; he is shown throughout as a fool and a coward.

The sacrifice is destined never to be completed. Aristophanes uses a device which has been the basis of innumerable music-hall acts, that of constant interruption. Pisthetairus is disturbed at his mock-devotions by one character after another intruding on some ridiculous errand. First comes a poet, insistent on reciting an epic poem he has composed in honour of the new city. He refuses to go until he is handsomely rewarded for his pains. Pisthetairus sends him packing with a gift of clothes borrowed from one of the chorus, but no sooner has he gone than a soothsayer bobs up in his place. He reads oracles which, so he claims, concern Cloudcuckooland ; their tenor is that the soothsayer should receive a present. By this time Pisthetairus' patience is exhausted, and he drives him off the stage, beating him vigorously as he goes. Then come, in rapid succession, Meton, a well-known architect with a town-planning project, a District Commissioner sent from Athens to administer the new state, and a statute-monger to sell it laws. The last two drive Pisthetairus to distraction between them, running in from opposite sides of the stage to threaten or wheedle. At last he gives up the sacrifice in disgust and leaves the stage.

The chorus make a mock proclamation. They offer a handsome reward for Philocrates the bird-seller, to be captured dead or alive. Then they step forward to address the judges who are to decide which play wins the festival, in a shameless appeal for votes.

> A word to our judges, on where to award the prize.
> If you vote for us, then all good things are yours,
> Gifts richer far than those of Alexander.
> First of all, what every critic sets his heart on —
> The owls on silver coins will never leave you
> But settle down for life inside your purses,
> Produce a family, and hatch small change.
> On top of that, your houses will be temples —
> We'll crown the gables of your roof with eagles.
> If you're a civil servant on the make,
> We'll put a little hawk into your hands
> That grabs as quick as lightning. When you're dining
> We'll give you a crop like ours, to store the food in.

As before, these humorous passages are mixed with beautiful lyrics.

O happy winged race of birds
That never in scorching summer weather
Pant in the sun's remorseless rays,
And cloakless face the winter days
Without an extra feather.

Our home is in the vaulted trees
And in the flowering meadows,
And when the heat-mad crickets cry
Shrill songs of blazing noon, we fly
To court the mid-day shadows.

We winter in the hollow caves
And join the mountain nymphs in play,
On snow-white myrtle berries browse
And perch among the Graces' flowers
In their gardens all the day.

Pisthetairus returns, to receive news that the wall has been completed. Almost immediately a sentry arrives in haste — one of the gods has already penetrated their defences and flown into the city. Pisthetairus is furious. There is immediate confusion. The birds run here and there, preparing to resist attack : Pisthetairus stands on the stage shouting orders; and, above their heads, the crane appears, carrying a figure wrapped in billowing draperies. It is Iris, the messenger of Olympus, Goddess of Rainbows. Pisthetairus jumps about trying to catch her as she is lowered to the stage. She is seized and cross-examined. It appears that the gods are already feeling the effect of the heavenly blockade, and Iris is on her way to order mankind to renew the sacrifices. Pisthetairus explains the new situation in forcible terms, and drives her off.

From this point the chorus take a less significant part in the play, only singing short topical verses between scenes and joining in the finale. One feels that Aristophanes has exhausted his power of invention in the wonderful choruses of the first half of the play, and can find nothing new for them to say in the second. The remaining verses are neatly written, but deal almost entirely in personalities. One, for example —

> Near the Shadow-footed People
> Lies a lake where filthy Socrat-
> es invokes the dead by magic,
> There Peisander paid a visit,
> Hoping to behold the spirit
> That had vanished from his body,
> With a camel-lamb to slaughter.
> There he slit the throat, departed
> Like Odysseus from the carcass.
> Up from underground directly
> To the body of the camel
> Chaerephon the Bat ascended.

has all the punch and polish of a modern revue number, but needs more knowledge than the average reader can supply to be fully appreciated.

A messenger enters. He has just returned from earth, and reports that people are full of enthusiasm for the new bird-city. Many have adopted birds' names. This gives occasion for more topical humour where even scholarship is unable to assist, as many of the people referred to are not mentioned elsewhere in literature. He concludes by saying that a large number of immigrants are arriving, and warns Pisthetairus to prepare for them.

Once more the stage is a scene of bustle and movement. A stage-hand summoned by Pisthetairus (a familiar comic device, as we have seen) rushes to and fro with hampers and boxes full of wings and feathers to fit out the newcomers. He is urged on by Pisthetairus and the chorus, who abuse him soundly for his slackness. Then a second procession of rascals begins. The first is a son who wants to kill his father and inherit the family property. He has heard that among the birds this is permissible. Pisthetairus agrees, but counters with another bird-law :

> When father stork has reared his little ones
> From fledglings and instructed them to fly,
> The chicks must care for father in their turn.

He persuades the young man to join the army and divert his fighting spirit into more orthodox channels.

Next comes Cinesias, a choral poet. This scene is strongly reminiscent of the scene with the poet in the first half of the play, with Cinesias insisting on reciting his bad verse until driven off with a beating. Third and last comes an informer, a well-known Athenian type frequently satirized on the comic stage. He makes his living by serving summonses and engaging in private lawsuits against those who have committed some civil offence. He wants a pair of racing wings to get about his business faster, and to make sure of the verdict before the defendant can get to court. Pisthetairus promises him a fine pair of wings, which turn out to be a whip.

Prometheus, the Titan who bestowed on man the god's jealously guarded fire — we have already seen him as the subject of a tragedy — now appears with a warning. His entry is the opposite of tragic. He is wrapped up so tight in his cloak that he cannot hear a word that is said to him, and carries a large parasol which he carefully keeps between him and heaven. This heavy disguise is to hide him from the gods. With difficulty persuaded to unwrap, he tells Pisthetairus that the gods are starving, and have been

forced to send a deputation to ask for peace. He is not to
yield unless Zeus restores his sceptre to the birds, and gives
his daughter Sovereignty to be his wife. Pisthetairus asks
who Sovereignty is, and Prometheus replies with typical
Aristophanic anti-climax :

> A lovely girl, who guards his thunderbolt,
> And everything he has — politic counsel,
> And law and order, wisdom, and the dockyards,
> Slander, wastepaper men and threepenny pieces.

Three gods make up the deputation. The Triballian
is a barbarian god, and speaks pidgin Greek. When asked
his opinion, he can only reply in a flow of unintelligible
gibberish. He has little to do, apart from providing the
excuse for a pun ('Triballians, the source of tribulation').
The Greeks found foreigners as funny as the English stage
does — the comic foreigner of Greek comedy is the comic
Frenchman of English farce. Tastes in humour alter little
over the centuries. The second ambassador, Heracles, is
more prominent. He was also a well-known and highly
popular comic figure. He is represented as a bully and a
glutton, all brawn and no brains. We possess terra-cotta
statuettes of this character, sucking his thumb with an
oafish smile or eating greedily. The audience at the *Birds*
would have greeted his appearance with a knowing laugh
— it was clear what turn the comedy would take now.

The third member of the divine trio is Poseidon, God
of Oceans. He is represented as pompous and over-
bearing ; though not as broad a figure of fun as the others,
he is treated with scant respect. Pisthetairus receives the
embassy with a show of indifference. He is busy cooking,
and takes more interest in his kitchen than in anything
they may have to say. Heracles is immediately attracted

by the prospect of food. There follows a hilarious scene of negotiations, with Heracles ready to sacrifice principle for his stomach, and the Triballian unable to understand a word anyone says. Only Poseidon is firmly opposed to Pisthetairus' proposals, and he is forced to submit by the indifference of the others.

Comedies normally end with a revel, procession or banquet, and this is no exception. Pisthetairus comes down from heaven with his new bride Sovereignty, and the chorus greet him with a wedding song :

> To Hera on Olympus' height
> The Fates conducted Heaven's Lord
> Of lofty throne, and at their rite
> Sang out this hymn in one accord.
> > Hymen, O Hymenaeus,
> > O Hymen, Hymenaeus.
>
> Love that makes all things to grow
> Attended at their marriage bed,
> Gave rein to their desires, and so
> Were Zeus and happy Hera wed.
> > Hymen, O Hymenaeus,
> > O Hymen, Hymenaeus.

Pisthetairus and the birds have won. He now holds all the attributes of Zeus.

> I love your wedding-hymns and love your song
> And revel in your words. Take now
> The infernal thunder that to Zeus belongs
> And lock the dreadful lightning up below,
> This too, the thunderbolt that terrifies,
> The fiery-tailed destroyer of the skies.

CHORUS.   Awful golden lightning flash,
> God's immortal fiery spear,
> Thunder that with hellish clash
> Makes rain-torrents to appear,

By the power that lies in this
He may rule both land and sea,
Zeus's empire, all is his,
And his handmaid, Sovereignty.

The *Birds* has all the virtues and failings of Greek comedy at its most typical. It is loose and episodic, a mixture of traditional elements and new material. The principal character provides a tenuous link between successive short scenes of varying relevance to the plot. The plot development itself is without logic. Sovereignty, for example, is introduced arbitrarily near the end merely to provide the traditional finale. There is no place in comedy for the tragic virtues of strict control and economy of material. This irrelevance has a close modern parallel in pantomime, where all the laws of logic are suspended — the Broker's Men appear in Prince Charming's ball to indulge in a juggling act, and Robin Hood leads his merry men in the latest popular song. There is a tendency to repetition ; the two poet scenes, for example, are almost identical. Characters are introduced arbitrarily and dropped without excuse. This was largely due to the fact that only a few actors were available to play a large number of parts, but no trouble is taken to make the changes plausible. Pisthetairus' companion, Euelpides, carries most of the action in the early part of the play, and Pisthetairus hardly says a word ; then Euelpides vanishes without reason or excuse, and is not heard of again.

Yet this sort of criticism is unfair. We must not expect a well-made play. What comedy lacks in economy it gains in scope, and gives opportunity for comment on every aspect of life. Springing from the carefree revels of a gay people, it provides an uninhibited parade of comic characters and incidents. It is easy to criticize from the austere view-point of the study, but the study is the last place to appreciate Greek comedy. We have seen how much of the humour is lost because of its topicality, but this is only a small proportion of the whole. The wonder is that so much of it has survived. As well as amusing us, Greek comedy provides an invaluable commentary on the daily life and foibles of a great people, not the considered deductions of historians and philosophers but the everyday chatter of the common man going about his business, recorded and transmuted by one of the greatest comic writers of his own or of any age.

CHAPTER IX

ROMAN COMEDY: PLAUTUS AND THE *MENAECHMI*

WHEN the Romans conquered Greece they took over many of its arts. 'Vanquished Greece', says Horace, 'subdued its savage captor.' Early Rome had developed literary traditions of its own, rough and unpolished but with a crude vigour that would have developed with time. Faced with the finished products of Greek culture this native tradition quickly succumbed. Greek influence pervaded the arts of the Roman empire for centuries. At best, it inspired enduring masterpieces, at worst, pallid imitations.

By the time the Romans arrived, Greek comedy had travelled a long way from the freedom enjoyed by Aristophanes. Absolute freedom of speech can only exist when the state is secure. The Athenian democracy at the peak of its power could afford to tolerate public criticism of the state, its leaders, institutions and gods. This was a mark of strength. Weak and unstable governments could not risk being laughed at. Less tolerant because less secure, they drove the old freedom from the stage. We have seen this influence at work in the plays of Aristophanes. When he wrote *Lysistrata* in 411, Athens was seething with political discontent. Rival factions were struggling for power and resorting to compulsion.

There was constant intrigue and negotiation. Not for a century had there been such turmoil within the city. Yet there is not one word of this in the *Lysistrata*. Aristophanes had learnt his unpleasant lesson. If he was to survive as a writer he must limit his genius.

So comedy sought new channels. It played for safety by using non-personal themes and abandoned its virulent attack on current problems for a gentle comedy of manners. It dealt with types rather than individuals, and its plots were calculated to give offence to no-one. Stage satire has always had a precarious existence. Molière was only able to indulge himself freely because he enjoyed royal patronage. In eighteenth-century England the stage had been an effective medium of political satire. It frequently offered pointed, scurrilous attacks on members of the Government. In 1737 Walpole, indignant at being thus pilloried in public, agitated to such an effect that plays were forbidden performance without the Lord Chamberlain's approval. Thus the office of Censor was instituted, which has endured to this day.

Menander, the only Greek poet of the New Comedy whose work has survived in quantity, has already been mentioned. Enough fragments exist of two of his plays, the *Arbitration* and the *Rape of the Locks*, for the plots to be reconstructed, and scholars have tried to fill the gaps by writing in the missing dialogue. The plots are slight — the *Arbitration* turns on the identity of an abandoned baby, claimed by two contending parties, and the *Rape of the Locks* is a case of supposed infidelity. A lady has had her head shorn in punishment for associating with a strange young man, who afterwards turns out to be her brother.

In the Georgian theatre we find characters neatly labelled according to their functions — 'heavy father', 'comic countryman', 'first walking gentleman' and so forth. Dickens describes a typical touring company in *Nicholas Nickleby*.

There was present a slim young gentleman with weak eyes, who played the low-spirited lovers and sang tenor songs, and who had come arm in arm with the comic gentleman — a man with a turned-up nose, large mouth, broad face and staring eyes. Making himself very amiable to the infant phenomenon was an inebriated elderly gentleman in the last depths of shabbiness, who played the calm and virtuous old men ; and paying especial court to Mrs. Crummles was another elderly gentleman, a shade more respectable, who played the irascible old men — those funny fellows who have nephews in the army, and perpetually run about with thick sticks to compel them to marry heiresses. Besides these, there was a roving-looking person in a rough great-coat who strode up and down in front of the lamps, flourishing a dress-cane, and rattling away in an undertone with great vivacity for the amusement of an ideal audience. He was not quite so young as he had been, and his figure was rather running to seed ; but there was an air of exaggerated gentility about him, which bespoke the hero of swaggering comedy.

Most plays fitted into this rigid scheme of type-casting. This made it easy to allot parts, but stifled imagination and invention in the playwright unless he was talented enough to override the limitations. In just such a way the Greek New Comedy could type its characters as 'Angry old man', 'Humorous old man', 'Young lover', 'Comic slave', 'Courtesan', and give each one its appropriate mask. An ancient authority gives a long list of such masks representing every type of part, and embodying subtle distinctions from which the audience could deduce the function of each character as he appeared.

New Comedy discovered the theme of romantic love, which does not appear in Aristophanes, though there are traces of it in the tragedies ; Antigone in Sophocles' play is loved by Haemon, the son of the man who condemns her to death, and there may have been a love-motif in Euripides' lost *Andromeda*. Love-plots form the basis of much of New Comedy — young love thwarted, old men's advances defeated, quarrels, reconciliations, happy endings. These situations were capable of infinite variation. A subsidiary and popular theme was that of mistaken identity. Long-lost sons and daughters are discovered, and marriage plots defeated by the discovery that the parties are related. Though the plots are artificial, they give scope for much humorous observation. They were widely acted both in existing theatres and on portable stages by touring companies. The chorus was by now divorced from the main action, and the new form of the theatre with its high stage gave the actors the prominence their new supremacy deserved.

Such was the wealth of dramatic material existing in Greece, and in the Greek colonies of South Italy. When the Romans extended their influence southwards, they found the plays waiting for them, and lost no time in taking them over wholesale. In the journey from Greece to Rome the plays suffered something of a sea-change. In rewriting, while retaining their Greek settings and a great deal of the Greek characterization, they became full of allusions to Roman affairs and customs. The slaves of Roman comedy, for example, address their masters with a freedom common enough among the Greeks, but which any Roman slave-owner worthy of his name would have punished immediately. A usual device of Roman writers was to combine the plots of two Greek comedies into one of their own, a process known as *contaminatio*. The plagiarism is mitigated by occasional 'credits' in the prologue — the original works and authors are sometimes mentioned. Comedy of this nature was known as *palliata*, 'comedy in the Greek dress'. As was natural, a reaction took place in the form of an alternative school, *comedia togata*, 'comedy in Roman dress', but no examples of this form survive.

The two authors of Roman comedy of whom complete plays survive are Plautus and Terence. We may deal briefly with Terence, though the later writer, first, Born about 185, he is said to have come to Rome from Carthage as a slave. Fortunate in finding a master who educated him and fostered his talents, he managed to earn the patronage of the fashionable literary clique of the time. The purity of his style has led some critics to credit these nobles with the authorship. Many of Terence's works are more moral problem-plays than comedies; some characters are seriously presented as deserving of sympathy, and the situations drawn with feeling. Worthy as this attitude was, it did not appeal to the Roman audiences. They demanded more robust entertainment. Terence complains in one prologue that they preferred dancers and rope-walkers to his comedies. His plays were above the popular taste of the time, though their elegance made them greatly appreciated by later generations. They were frequently acted in the Middle Ages, and read for centuries in schools until strict Victorian morality decreed that their subject-matter was unfit for the young.

The same cannot be said of his predecessor, Titus Maccius Plautus, born in 251 B.C. Plautus was a man of the people. He was also more wholly a man of the theatre than any of the Greek writers, in that he wrote plays for his living, thus depending on satisfying the public taste. Tradition has it that he acquired some capital from his work in the theatre, only to lose it later. Poverty forced him to work in a flour-mill, where he wrote three plays. After that he never looked back. His work remained highly popular, and was performed long after his death. He was predominantly a translator, though none of his Greek originals have come down to us for comparison. However, he consistently enlivened his plots with topical allusions. All his plays are type-comedies — a familiar motivator of the plot is the parasite, a social hanger-on who flattered and paid lip-service to his patron in return for food and presents. The plays vary a great deal in tone. *Prisoners of War* tells with some pathos the story of an old man who finds his own son working for him as a slave. *Captain Vainglorious* has for its leading character that well-known theatrical type, the boastful soldier. *Buried Treasure*, from which Molière took *L'Avare*, portrays the agonies of a miser who thinks his hoard has been stolen. These plays, together with the *Menaechmi* (*The Menaechmus Brothers*), stand out from the rest, which are all-too-familiar stories of thwarted love, deluded old men and conniving slaves. Plautus was a prolific writer, and aimed at commercial success ; when he had found a popular formula, he stuck to it.

Plautus is no great literary figure, and for this reason is often underestimated. Of all the dramatists we have considered, he loses most through being read rather than seen. Great plays, like great music, work on the public in two ways. They have an immediate impact which comes with performance, but this, though overwhelming, is not enough. There is not time during the performance to consider all the dramatist's implications, to weigh arguments and appreciate nuances. This can only come later, by subsequent study and re-reading of the work. All the works of the Greek dramatists have something to offer at both levels, but Plautus off the stage is a fish out of water. Though he can occasionally conjure up a pithy epigram, and his versification is not without interest, he needs the actor's art to bring his plays to life. Much of his humour relies on the pun, notoriously unfunny unless well delivered. Anyone who has had the opportunity of comparing the script of a radio comedy programme with the lines as exactly spoken will have been amazed at how words, dull and humourless on paper, appear as pearls of wit when given the proper delivery and inflection. So it is with much of Plautus. Most of Aristophanes is funny to the reader ; most of Plautus is funny only to the audience.

Plautus' genius lies in his mastery of stage situation. He has an unerring eye for how to begin and end a scene. The action never falters, nor is it unduly prolonged by long speeches. Repartee is swift and pointed, and owes much to the vernacular. When long speeches and soliloquies are inserted, they always serve to advance the plot or add to our knowledge of the character. As a comedian Plautus has the great merit of knowing when to stop. Minor characters never outstay their welcome. He is content to let them play one or two short scenes, often extremely funny, and then firmly removes them, leaving the audience, as it should be, wanting more. The plays themselves are short, but into them he manages to pack an astonishing amount of comic contrivance. All is done so neatly, however, that the audience is never lost in the details of the plot. As works of stage craftsmanship the comedies are superb, and served as models for other writers for centuries. All these qualities are exemplified in the *Menaechmi*.

The Roman theatre was developed from the Greek, though without its effective simplicity. As in Greece the first theatres were of wood, later superseded by stone, which Roman fondness for the grandiose made ornate and over-elaborate. The stage was increased in size, and the orchestra reduced to a semicircle. We also have hints of new mechanical devices — shifting scenes, and a curtain to conceal the stage in the modern manner, rising from a slot in the ground instead of falling from the ceiling as to-day. Descriptions of these innovations are tantalizingly brief, and it is impossible to reconstruct their operation. Not content with building new theatres, the Romans imposed their pattern on existing theatres in Greece, cutting down the orchestra to their own requirements and remodelling the *skene*.

In later years the Roman theatre turned almost entirely towards spectacle, and stage buildings became larger and more elaborate still. When Plautus wrote, however, some of the Greek simplicity still remained. All his plays need is an architectural background, with doors to represent the houses of the principal characters; the action passes before these as in a street. Strangely, many details of the Roman performances are more obscure than those of the Greek. It is a matter of dispute, for example, whether or not the actors wore masks. The texts of the plays were divided into *diverbia* (spoken dialogue) and *cantica* (sung portions or recitatives). Thus the action was enlivened at intervals with music and song. The plots of Plautus, at least, are of the calibre of musical comedy, and it is in these terms that we can best appreciate him.

THE *MENAECHMI*

The plays of Plautus as found in the manuscripts are prefaced by prologues to be spoken by the manager or one of the company. These were almost certainly not written by Plautus. The *Menaechmi* prologue is not only unnecessary but infuriating, as it gives away the details of the plot in advance.

The scene is Epidamnus, and the first character to appear is the well-known parasite. His name, he tells us, is Peniculus, the 'Sponge', because he always wipes the table clean. He then launches himself on a philosophy of food.

If you ask me, men are very foolish to keep prisoners in chains, or clap runaway slaves in irons. When a man's in a bad way, and one trouble comes on top of another, he's all the more eager to do what's wrong and run away. They'll slip their chains somehow — file through the fetters, or smash the padlock with a stone, and think nothing of it. No : if you want to keep someone safe, and make sure he won't run away, bind him to you with food and drink. Set a good table and strap his snout to that. As long as you can wine him and dine him every day at his pleasure, till he's had enough, escape won't enter his head though he's condemned to death. You'll keep him easily as long as you use chains like that. A chain that never lets go, that's what a stomach is — the more you stretch it, the tighter it holds you.

Peniculus is a good example of his own philosophy. He is off to pay his patron, Menaechmus, a visit.

He doesn't just feed men, oh no ! It's an education, a new lease of life, to dine with him. That's the sort of young man he is. He has a colossal appetite himself and serves banquets fit for the gods, loads the tables, piles up the plates so high that you have to stand on a chair to reach the top. I haven't been to see him for some days now — no invitation ! I've been at home with my dear ones — there's nothing I eat or buy that doesn't come very dear indeed. But now my supply corps has deserted, and I'm going to see Menaechmus.

He has hardly finished speaking when he sees Menaechmus himself coming out of his house. Characters entering through the stage doors are commonly introduced by the tag '*concrepuit ostium*', 'the door creaked'. This draws the audience's attention to the entrance. Here, however, we hear more than the door creaking. Menaechmus is indulging in a violent and one-sided argument with his wife, whom we must imagine as just off-stage. He abuses her for watching his movements so carefully.

Every time I want to leave the house you call me back, keep me waiting, ask me questions : Where am I going ? What am I doing ? What's my business ? What am I taking from the house ? I've married a customs officer, not a wife.

Menaechmus is clearly that stock comic figure, the hen-pecked husband. On this occasion at least he intends to retaliate by taking another lady out to dinner. Peniculus, overhearing this threat, is appalled. If Menaechmus is eating out, his hopes of a free meal have vanished. Menaechmus soon ends his fears. Under his cloak he is wearing a woman's gown which he has stolen from his wife's wardrobe as a present for Erotium, the lady in question. He proposes to Peniculus that they take it to her and order dinner for the three of them. Peniculus, needless to say, is delighted, and is only prevented from beating on Erotium's door by the appearance of the lady herself. She accepts the gown with every mark of pleasure (to the accompaniment of some sarcastic asides from Peniculus), and promises to prepare dinner for them. Menaechmus and Peniculus leave to take a turn round the forum, while Erotium summons her cook and sends him shopping. The cook is alarmed at the news that Peniculus will be present — 'That makes ten guests ; the parasite can eat enough for eight'. He departs with his basket for the market-place. Erotium re-enters her house and the stage is left empty.

A new character now appears, followed by a slave and a number of sailors carrying baggage. At first it seems as if it is Menaechmus come back again, but from his conversation this cannot be the case — he has just come off a ship. We soon learn, however, that his name too is Menaechmus, and that he has come from Syracuse to Epidamnus in search of his long-lost twin brother. His slave, Messenio, is tired of travelling.

Then how much longer are we going to search for him ? It's six years now since we started — we've been to the Danube, Spain, the South of France, Illyria, the Greek colonies, and the whole coast of Italy wherever the sea can reach. If you'd been looking for a needle you'd have found it long ago, if there was one to find. We're looking for a dead man among the living. We should have found him long ago, if he were still alive.

This only earns him a sharp rebuke. But he has not done grumbling, and attacks from another angle by pointing out how little money they have.

Listen to me, Menaechmus. To look at our purse, we're only out for a summer excursion. If you ask me, unless you go home you'll be in no end of bother looking for your brother when everything's gone. As for the people that live here ! Epidamnus is the place where all the gay sparks and heavy drinkers come from ; this is where the confidence men live, and the parasites. And they say the street-women here are more seductive than anywhere else on earth. That's why it's called Epidamnus — because you're damned as soon as you set foot in the place.

Menaechmus' immediate reaction is to demand the purse with their travelling money.

You're a great one for the girls, Messenio, and I'm apt to lose my temper. I can't control myself. So if I keep it, I'll guard against both things — that you don't run off with it, and that I don't fly into a rage with you.

Messenio surrenders the wallet with a bad grace. Their conversation is interrupted by Erotium's cook, returning from the market with meat for dinner. Misled by the likeness, he mistakes this new Menaechmus for the other, and assumes that the guests are waiting for their meal before it is even cooked. So the complications begin. The cook approaches Menaechmus and is astonished to find that he claims not to know him. Eventually he puts it down to a joke, and goes in to cook dinner and tell Erotium that her guest is waiting. Erotium emerges, makes the same mistake, twines herself amorously round Menaechmus and tries to lead him in. When he refuses she grows indignant, and he, more and more puzzled as

she calls him by his name and seems to know his father
and his birthplace. In vain he insists that he only came to
Epidamnus by ship that very morning, and has never seen
her before in his life. It is a necessary convention of the
mistaken–identity plot that none of the characters realize
until the end of the play what anyone of normal intelli-
gence would see within two minutes. Though Menaechmus has come expressly in search of his twin brother, it
never crosses his mind that it may be that brother for
whom he is being mistaken ! Without this strange lack
of comprehension, however, there would be no play. So
we must put up with it as best we can.

Yielding to Messenio's insistent whispers, Menaechmus
gives him back their wallet, but determines to take advantage of the woman's mistake — 'I'll agree to anything she
says, if I can get a meal out of it !' Messenio does his best
to hold him back, but to no purpose. Menaechmus'
greed defeats his caution, and he allows Erotium to lead
him inside, determined to profit by this accident as much
as he can. Messenio, resigned to the inevitable, leads his
shipmates off to an inn where they can deposit their
baggage.

Peniculus comes running in, angry and out of breath.
He and his patron have been separated in the forum, and
Peniculus, under no illusions about his popularity, is con-
vinced that he has been given the slip so that Menaechmus
can have dinner without him. He curses the bad luck
that involved him in a meeting and so gave Menaechmus
the chance to escape.

Damnation on the man who invented meetings to take up
men's time when they're busy enough already ! It's no
occupation for gentlemen of leisure. There are plenty of men

who only eat once a day and have nothing to do — who neither get invitations nor give them. If things were run that way I shouldn't have lost to-day's dinner. I feel more like a corpse than a human being. But I'll go inside — even the thought of picking up the scraps is attractive.

He is too late. Menaechmus of Syracuse, having obviously wined and dined well, staggers out of Erotium's house, with a banqueter's wreath on his head. The plot thickens. Peniculus makes the same mistake as everyone else and assumes that his worst suspicions are confirmed. Menaechmus has indeed been lucky. Not only has he had a free meal, but Erotium has given him the gown she received earlier, to take to be remodelled. Menaechmus gladly accepts the commission, making his own reservations about what he will do with it. Peniculus is furious. He accosts his supposed patron and abuses him soundly.

What have you to say for yourself? You cheat, you shyster, you feather in the wind, you despicable worthless thief! What have I done to you, for you to ruin me? Why did you sneak away from the forum earlier on, and put away your dinner when I wasn't there? How did you dare? It was mine as much as yours!

So follows another scene of cross-purposes, Menaechmus highly indignant at being so addressed by a complete stranger, and Peniculus assuming that he is trying to disown him. At last he can stand it no longer, and goes off to punish him in the best way he knows by telling his wife about the stolen gown. Before Menaechmus can get away he is stopped by Erotium's maid bringing a bracelet she would like enlarged.

'Tell her the bracelet will come back with the gown,' says Menaechmus ambiguously, and goes off laughing to find his slave. To mislead possible pursuit he leaves his wreath as a false clue on the opposite side of the stage. He has had nothing but profit from the mistake ; it remains for his unfortunate double to pay for it.

Peniculus returns with his wife, a formidable matron fulminating over what she has been told. They find the dropped wreath and are just about to set off in pursuit when the unsuspecting victim enters. In a long speech he explains his absence, which left the coast clear for his brother to take his place, and comments acidly on the reasons for it. Here the atmosphere is purely Roman ; the customs and institutions to which Menaechmus refers owe nothing to the Greek original.

Our most treasured social custom is a tedious bore, and it's precisely those who are richest and most honoured by their fellow citizens who hold it in greatest respect. They all want to collect armies of clients. They never ask whether they're good men or rascals — their standing depends on something far more important than honesty. If a man's poor but respectable, he's a rogue ; if he's rich and a villain, he passes for an estimable client. They have no thought for the law, or for what's good and right, keep their patrons on tenterhooks, take things and swear they haven't ; they're avaricious, deceitful, always in court, and make their money by usury and lies. Their whole heart's in quarrelling. When the client appears in court the patron has to be there too. Just like to-day. A client gave me no end of trouble, and I wasn't free to choose my own actions or my own company. He hung on to me, wouldn't let me go. I had to plead for his dirty deeds before the bench in the hope of settling by asking for a payment of moneys into the court, making it difficult and complicated for the other party. I had said as much as I could, and what did my client do ? What ? Demanded a trial, and I've never seen a man more obviously guilty.

He decides to go in, late as it is, and enjoy his postponed dinner-party, secure in the knowledge that Erotium's good humour has been assured by the present of the gown. At this his wife and Peniculus step out of hiding and confront him. He has to admit his theft, though only after a great many prevarications and excuses, but cannot understand how he has offended Peniculus. His repeated assertions that he has only just returned and so cannot have dined meet with disbelief — Peniculus has the evidence of his own eyes. His wife sweeps indoors, warning him that he will not be allowed home without the gown, and Peniculus, his credit with the family exhausted, disappears. Menaechmus crosses the stage to Erotium's house. Calling her out, he asks her to return the gown. She, of course, insists that he already has it, and when he persists, assumes that he is trying to cheat her, and orders him out of her house. Menaechmus is completely bewildered by this strange turn of events. 'She's gone in and locked the door. I'm the most shut-out man that ever was. I'm a liar at home and a liar to my mistress. I'll go and ask my friends what they think I ought to do.'

So he goes, leaving the stage conveniently clear for Menaechmus of Syracuse. He has by now recovered from the effects of the dinner, but still carries the gown. The wife, eagerly looking out for her husband's return, sees him and makes the inevitable mistake. She harangues him for his bad behaviour, while he, perplexed at being attacked again by a complete stranger, replies in kind, to such effect that she sends for her father to give her support. The old man totters in, complaining about the effects of old age and the propensity of married couples to quarrel.

I'll put my best foot foremost when I have to, and try to get along as well as my age will let me. But it isn't easy, make no mistake. All the hurry's gone out of me : the years have withered me up ; my body's a burden, my strength's disappeared. Old age is a bad business, bad for the back, and brings all sorts of troubles when it comes. If I went through the list I'd never stop talking. But what's on my mind to worry me at the moment is, why did my daughter send for me in such a hurry ? She's given me no idea what she wants or why she's called me. But I'm pretty sure what the trouble is. She's had a quarrel with her husband. That's what they're like, the shrews, relying on their money to keep their husbands under their thumb. And in most cases the man isn't blameless either. There's a limit to letting a wife have her own way.

His suspicions are justified. Peering across the stage, he sees the wife in tears and Menaechmus indignant in a corner. He is testy and impatient, with firm ideas on the responsibility of marriage, seen from the husband's point of view.

Haven't I told you time and time again to put up with your husband's ways and turn a blind eye to where he goes and what he does there ? . . . What do you want to go poking your nose in for ? You might as well pretend you can stop him dining out or asking his friends home. Do you think husbands were made to wait on you ? Do you want to keep him tied to your apron strings, or make him sit among your maids winding wool ? . . . As long as he does the right thing by you, and keeps you in clothes, and servants, and wool to spin, it's far better to be sensible, my girl.

But even his prejudice yields before his daughter's complaint that her husband is stealing her things for another woman. He goes over to have it out with him, and Menaechmus, persecuted by yet another complete stranger, is more angry than ever. Father and daughter come to the conclusion that he is mad. Menaechmus seizes on this as his one chance of escape — 'If they think I'm mad, the best thing I can do is pretend I am, and scare them off'. So he pretends to be divinely possessed, and in a richly farcical scene rushes round the stage as though listening to a voice from heaven. The voice, apparently, tells him in no uncertain terms how to deal with the persecutors.

> Ahoy, Bacchus ! Oh, Bromius,
> Where dost thou bid me to hunt in the woods?
> I hear thy voice but cannot stir from hence —
> A raving bitch doth guard me on the left
> And on the right a balding aged goat
> Who many a time and oft hath cost
> An innocent man his cause through perjury!
> Apollo's oracle commands me now
> With flaming torches to burn out her eyes!

His feigned madness and eventual collapse have the desired effect. First the wife and then her father run away, the latter to fetch a doctor. Menaechmus is at last free to make his escape to his ship, hissing an aside to the audience as he goes — 'If the old man comes back, don't tell him which way I've gone'.

The old man returns, dragging a doctor with him. This is another splendidly written part, a sustained parody of the professional manner. Our attitude to doctors has altered since the last century, the profession becoming more dignified in public esteem. Before this, their professional jargon, mysterious attitude and ambiguous status made them popular butts. Molière, who satirized the medical profession so penetratingly in *Le Médecin malgré lui*, *Monsieur de Porceaugnac* and *Le Malade imaginaire*, would have sympathized with Plautus' portrait of the Roman doctor here. He catches the other Menaechmus still wandering about with nowhere to go. The scene of the medical examination is worth quoting in full.

DOCTOR. How are you, Menaechmus? Dear me, why have you uncovered your arm? Don't you know how much it aggravates the disease?

MENAECHMUS. Why don't you go hang yourself?

OLD MAN. What do you think?

DOCTOR. What don't I think! Hellebore's no use in this case. Now, now, Menaechmus!

MENAECHMUS. What do you want?

DOCTOR. Answer my questions, please. Do you take your wine black?

MENAECHMUS. Go to the devil.

OLD MAN. That's his madness coming on.

MENAECHMUS. Why not ask whether I eat purple bread or yellow bread, or red bread if it comes to that! Or if I eat birds with scales or fish with feathers!

OLD MAN. Oh dear, oh dear, do you hear how he's raving? What are you waiting for? Give him some medicine before he has a fit.

DOCTOR. Just a moment. I have more questions to ask.

OLD MAN. This talk will be the death of him.

DOCTOR. Tell me, are your eyes ever swollen?

MENAECHMUS. What do you think I am, you clown, a grasshopper?

DOCTOR. Tell me, does your stomach ever rumble, eh?

MENAECHMUS. When I'm full, no ; when I'm empty, yes.

DOCTOR. He doesn't sound like a madman. Do you have a good night's rest? Do you drop off to sleep easily?

MENAECHMUS. When I've no debts on my conscience. Confound you for a busybody.

DOCTOR. Now he's starting to rave. Watch out when he talks like that.

OLD MAN. He's talking better than he was before — he called his wife a mad bitch!

MENAECHMUS. I said what?

OLD MAN. You were mad, I tell you.

MENAECHMUS. Me?

OLD MAN. Yes, you! You threatened to run me down with a four-horse chariot, I saw you; I tell you, that's what you did.

MENAECHMUS. And I know you stole Jupiter's sacred wreath; and I know you were put in prison for it; and I know you were flogged when they let you out; and I know you killed your father and sold your mother. Satisfied? Have I slandered you as much as you slandered me?

His heavy sarcasm is taken by the others for the last stages of delirium, and they decide to send slaves to carry him off to the doctor's house. Menaechmus, not hearing this, is only too pleased at finding himself alone, and unwisely decides to stay where he is.

It must now be assumed to be evening, for Messenio returns as ordered to meet his master where he left him. He does not see the other Menaechmus at first, but indulges in a characteristic monologue on the duties of a slave, the first of which is self-preservation.

You can tell a good slave by whether he sees to his master's affairs, looks after things, keeps them in order and uses his brains, and when he protects his master's interests in his absence as well as when he's on the spot, or better. If he knows his place, he ought to think more of his back than his gullet, and more of his legs than his belly. He should remember the rewards idle, thieving good-for-nothings get from their masters — beatings, chains, the treadmill, exhaustion, cold, starvation. That's what comes of laziness. It's my great fear. I don't mind what's said to me, but I hate being beaten, and would rather have my corn ground for me than grind it for others. So I obey my master's orders and serve him well and discreetly — I conduct myself so as to keep my back in one piece, and I'm better for it. Others can do as they like,

I'll do what I ought to. If I stick to that I'll keep out of trouble. As long as I'm ready whenever he wants me I shan't have much to fear. It's nearly time for him to repay me for my services.

As he finishes speaking, the old man hustles on the slaves who are to take Menaechmus to the doctor. Nervously they approach their unsuspecting victim, edging behind him as he sits mournfully at the side of the stage. He is carried off, kicking and protesting. Messenio is roused by his shouts for help and naturally takes him to be his master. He rushes to his defence, and a spirited fight ensues ; Menaechmus and Messenio take on the four slaves, kicking, biting and gouging, and drive them off. Menaechmus is full of gratitude, and Messenio takes this favourable opportunity to ask for what every slave desired, his liberty. Menaechmus is puzzled again — he has no power to grant this request ; Messenio is no slave of his. Messenio takes this for assent, and goes off over-joyed to fetch the money and luggage, while Menaechmus nerves himself for another attempt to recover his wife's gown from Erotium.

Messenio returns as quickly as he went, followed by his real master, Menaechmus of Syracuse. They are arguing bitterly. Menaechmus is outraged at his slave's claim to liberty, while Messenio naturally thinks that his master has repented of his generosity and is trying to go back on his promise. As they quarrel, Menaechmus of Epidamnus is driven once more from Erotium's house, still unable to understand what is going on. For the first time the brothers are on stage together, and it only remains to make clear to the characters in the play what the audience has known from the beginning.

So far Plautus' control of his material has been admirable. Each successive scene has been a variation on the theme of mistaken identity, but each has had a difference, and been given some new twist. Nothing has been overdone. The final recognition scene, however, is so prolonged that we begin to wonder whether even the Menaechmus brothers can have been so stupid. Recognition scenes have been a recurrent problem for dramatists over the centuries. They vary between the incredibly rapid, as in Molière's *Les Fourberies de Scapin*, where two pairs of long-separated fathers and daughters are reunited in the space of a few lines, or the protracted and tedious, as in Shakespeare's *All's Well that Ends Well* where complication after complication prolongs the inevitable outcome beyond endurance. In this play Plautus parades the facts we already know, not once but twice. Messenio conducts an examination which finally convinces the brothers of their relationship. The day's mistakes are explained to their mutual satisfaction, and they go off happily together. Messenio is left with the task of auctioning the property of the Epidamnian twin, and ends the play with an announcement to the audience :

Oyez! Oyez! Menaechmus will hold an auction on the morning of to-day week. Sale of slaves, furniture, estate and property! Everything to go to the highest bidder, ready money only! Sale of wife too, if anyone wants to buy her! Now good-bye, audience — and give us a good clap!

This final appeal for applause was as regular a closure of Roman comedy as the appeal for the prize was of Greek. We may hope that the audience responded, for in this case at least it was deserved.

The *Menaechmi*, like most of Plautus, is at best good music-hall. The characters lack depth, the dialogue is without that brilliance we associate with works of an earlier epoch. Yet it is the best of its kind; as farce, it is consistently and satisfyingly funny. The measure of Plautus' success with his material may be seen by comparing the play with a later imitation. There was an Italian version, *The Twins from Sicily*, by the prolific author Goldoni, and in England the plot fell into the hands of Shakespeare, who modelled his *Comedy of Errors* closely on Plautus. Shakespeare introduced further complications in the shape of two sets of twins, the brothers Antipholus and the two Dromios. All four were born on the same day, and the parents of the Antipholi marked this remarkable coincidence by giving their sons the Dromios as servants. As in Plautus, one Antipholus, with his Dromio, is lost, and when the play opens lives in Ephesus. The appearance in that city of the corresponding brothers begins a chain of mistakes whose mathematical permutations seem inexhaustible. In Shakespeare we soon give up the unequal struggle of trying to remember which twin is which — the only guiding principle is that it is bound to be the wrong one. In Plautus the humour is increased by the author's never leaving us in doubt as to which twin is on the stage. Not only do their introductory remarks at each new entrance establish their identity, but they are well differentiated in character. Menaechmus of Epidamnus is slow and pompous, with a ponderous delight in his marital peccadilloes. He is well suited to be the butt of the piece. His brother is sharper, with a keen eye to his own advantage. Though equally baffled, he is quick to see where profit lies.

The theme of identical twins has provided amusement for centuries. It was old when Plautus used it, and has been used by writers of comedy from him to Anouilh. Plautus' play has even been turned into a musical film, *The Boys from Syracuse*. In one form or another it will continue to delight audiences for centuries to come. Messenio's appeal for 'a good clap' should never fail of its effect.

CHAPTER X

PROBLEMS OF TRANSLATION

EVEN the briefest account of the Greek drama would be incomplete without some words on the only means by which it can be known to the majority of its readers. With the decline of classical studies, translation ceased to be a mildly amusing literary exercise and became an art in its own right. It is the translator's task to bridge the gap of centuries and inspire in the modern public the same emotions that the works aroused in the Greeks at first performance. Thus he is in the unique position of being both audience and creator. He must be alive to every implication of the original and have the art to convey them to others in terms they will understand. It is a difficult and responsible position. Too often translation becomes a distorting glass through which only occasional glimpses of the original are visible. Many are attracted to translation without the necessary qualifications. The poet with an exquisite feeling for words but insufficient scholarship may produce work beautiful in itself but with little relation to the original. This is the fault of Ezra Pound's translations, which achieve an occasional striking image at the cost of elementary schoolboy howlers. The scholar who knows the author and his period may produce a translation which is arid and uninteresting, and leaves the reader wondering why the work should ever have been called great. Nevertheless pure scholarship can often, by emendation or elucidation, reveal new beauties in a familiar text.

Translation has been likened to a woman : if beautiful, not faithful ; if faithful, not beautiful. All translation is difficult, that of drama more so, and that of Greek drama most of all. The depressing truth about work in this field is that while one may achieve either a good translation or a good play, it is almost impossible to combine them. He who attempts it runs the risk of falling heavily between two stools. This is due to the peculiar flexibility of the Greek language. It has been said that writing in Greek is like moulding in clay, writing in Latin like carving in marble. The same applies to Greek and English. Greek is a highly inflected language. The English noun has two cases and two numbers, the Greek five and three ; the English verb two voices, the Greek three. Greek uses particles to express many different shades of meaning which English can only convey by lengthy and elaborate periphrasis. What Greek can say in one line may need two or three in English.

This presents enormous difficulties. To convey the full meaning, the English must expand and elaborate, but this conflicts with the requirements of the dramatic form. Elaboration kills the drama. A play's impact must be immediate. Words pass quickly over the audience's heads. If they lose the thread of the argument they cannot turn back and start again, as in a book. This may come later, with publication — one cannot expect to grasp the author's every implication, any more than to understand the complexities of a Beethoven quartet, at one sitting. But something must come through or the play is a failure.

Every line must carry a punch, every sentence have its point. Drown the play in a welter of words and the audience will be confused and irritated. Drama cannot afford to be discursive. A playwright can permit himself three words for the philosopher's dozen, or a sentence to stand for a paragraph.

Applying these criteria to translation, we see that whatever happens something must be forfeited. If we concentrate on conveying the full implications of the Greek and reproducing every fine shade of meaning, the play loses impact. If we try to preserve the force and attack necessary to stimulate an audience, we must concentrate on the principal meaning to the exclusion of all others, thus over-simplifying the author's thought and, inevitably, misleading. A translation must be either frankly literary or frankly dramatic. Many fail to realize this and try to act the one and read the other. The prevalence of literary translations in the past has created an impression that Greek drama is dull and prosy. Nothing could be further from the truth.

Translation is, however, an acid test of verbosity. In the *Frogs* Euripides defends his prologues against those of Aeschylus. 'If you find any irrelevancy', he says, 'or any repetitiveness, any padding, you may spit on me.' The same is not true of all his choruses. Euripides with his new approach to tragic writing often gives the impression of finding the choruses tiresome. He takes one thought or sentiment and dresses it up in a variety of ways, expressing the same meaning several times in different language. The beauty and infinite variability of Greek disguise this lack of content, but in translation we find that once the manner has been shed there is too little matter. The translator is forced to find some way of reproducing Euripides' repetitions in a language ill suited to such devices. No translation can convey the whole of its original, but the proportion that can be conveyed is as good a test as any of the play's greatness. As time, by a process of the survival of the fittest, preserves only the greatest and most memorable works for posterity — though it may have lost many works of genius, it has kept surprisingly little trash — so translation has a way of revealing the true value of its originals by eliminating the superficial graces.

Some years ago France sent a diplomatic telegram to the United States, 'La France demande une réponse'. Translated 'France demands an answer', this nearly caused an international incident. The true meaning, of course, was much milder, 'France asks for an answer', but force of association led to an elementary mistake. If such misconceptions can arise between two living languages, what can we expect in translating from the language of an age long past, whose social and religious structure, culture and background were so different from our own ? Each word carries with it its own train of associations, differing widely between one language and another. The literary translator may fall back on notes at the end of the book, but this is denied to translations for the stage. Greek dramatists often used words in such a way that their habitual associations and implications coloured the whole context. How is this to be conveyed to an English audience for whom the corresponding word has either no associations or very different ones ? A typical case is the Greek word *xenos*, variously translated as 'stranger', 'guest' or 'friend' according to context. There is no particular significance here for the Englishman, but for the Greek it denoted an important code of social behaviour. As is still the case among the Arabs, and to some extent in Greece to-day, laws of hospitality were paramount. A stranger had the right to demand fair treatment. In the passage from the *Cyclops* quoted earlier, Odysseus, threatened with death, protests that the Cyclops has violated these rights :

> It is law among men, and custom demands it,
> That castaways craving for kindness and shelter
> Should depart dry-apparelled, with presents in their packs.

This hospitality once offered and accepted established a relationship sanctified by religion. To break it by deceit or treachery on either side was a violation of divine law. So when Hecuba, in Euripides' play of that name, tells us that she has entrusted her son Polydorus for safety to her old *xenos* Polymestor, the audience, who have already seen Polydorus' ghost and know that Polymestor has killed him for his money, appreciate that a sin has been committed deserving the most terrible retribution. This sense is completely lacking in English. The usual expedient of elaborating the meaning of *xenos* by translating 'guest-friend' is merely clumsy, and goes no further towards solving the problem.

A problem arising in all languages is that of translating puns and plays on words. Here it is particularly difficult because of the significance of the pun in Greek. Punning has had a curious and fluctuating history. It is a form of that rich association which is an essential part of poetry ; so, broadly speaking, the age of poetry loved it while the age of reason despised it. Puns and verbal conceits play an important part in Shakespeare and his fellow Elizabethans. In the succeeding age a reaction took place, typified by Johnson's comment, 'The pun was Shake-speare's fatal Cleopatra, for which he lost the world and was content to lose it'. Jane Austen, in *Mansfield Park*, makes one of her characters exclaim in horror, 'I hope you will not suspect me of a pun!' In the later nineteenth century the pendulum swung the other way, and the pun was a legitimate and highly appreciated form of humour. Hood could write poems consisting of nothing else:

> Ben Battle was a soldier bold
> And used to war's alarms.
> But a cannon ball took off his legs,
> So he laid down his arms ;

while à Beckett's *Comic Histories* use the pun almost exclusively for their humour. With the present century it fell once more into disrepute, and is only now being restored to favour by the writings of dramatists like Christopher Fry. The Greeks saw a mystic significance in the pun. In those days there was no scientific study of philology. That two words should resemble each other could only convey some divine intention. In Euripides' *Bacchantes* the King of Thebes is Pentheus, a name closely resembling *penthos*, 'sorrow'. This unhappy likeness is commented upon as an ominous portent of things to come. In translation the pun is lost and the casual reader left wondering what the characters are talking about. In *Agamemnon* the chorus revile Helen as 'Helen, the destroyer of ships, destroyer of men, destroyer of cities' with a play on the name Helene and the root *hel* — 'destroy'. What remains of this in translation ? Attempts to keep it, like Headlam's 'Helen, Hell enough she proved', can only strike a humorous note fatal in this context, because the English mind sees the pun as a joke and a bad joke at that.

In comedy, needless to say, word-play good, bad and indifferent abounds. Sometimes it is irrelevant and can safely be omitted or glossed over without damaging the play's structure, but what can be done when the argument turns on it ? In the *Birds* the chorus pervert etymology to emphasize their importance to mankind. They demonstrate how the Greek for 'bird', *ornis*, has acquired many other meanings — sneeze, omen, donkey. It is meaningless to reproduce this joke literally. The translator must convey the spirit rather than the words, and rewrite his original. Fortunately the word 'bird' has many proverbial and vernacular uses in English — 'the early bird catches the worm', 'a bird in the hand', 'to get the bird' — and a number of these may be substituted for Aristophanes' list. Though the words are different, the sense remains.

Some of Aristophanes' puns have stretched translators' ingenuity to its utmost. In the *Birds* again, the wren is stated to have been the first created thing, born even before the earth. Thus when her father died she had nowhere to bury him ! After much pondering she eventually buried him 'in Cephaleia'. The joke here lies in the resemblance between Cephaleia, a district of Athens, and *cephalē*, 'head'. Customary translations on the lines of 'on the crest of a headland' are weak. It was left to the Victorian translator, B. B. Rogers, who had an enviable knack for these problems, to translate by 'Bury St. Hedmunds'.

The form of the translation presents further problems. The relative merits of verse and prose versions have been keenly argued. Prose has recently become more popular. It is advocated by publishers of translations for the general public ; they believe, perhaps rightly, that the general

reader will accept a prose play more readily than one in
verse. It is true that many will jib, albeit unconsciously,
at anything smacking of 'poetry', and, offered the choice
between a prose and a verse work, will unhesitatingly
choose the former. This method may increase sales, and
is valuable in bringing the Greek drama to a public who
would otherwise never hear of it. Its value to the plays
is more dubious. The form and language of Greek
drama are highly artificial — here again the distinction
between realistic and non-realistic in art becomes important
— and it is dangerous to attempt to reproduce them in
the forms of everyday speech. There is an inevitable inconsistency between matter and form. Also, a new reader
coming to a Greek tragedy set out in the form of a modern
play may be misled into judging it by inappropriate
standards. The same problem exists in music. There is a
strong modern tendency to adapt the work of classical
composers to modern lyrics and popular presentation.
This may make a few themes better known, but does
nothing to increase the appreciation of the original.

A verse translation is, on the whole, to be desired. As
far as speeches and dialogue are concerned the form
presents little difficulty. The usual Greek line, as we have
seen, was the iambic trimeter. The English iambic pentameter gives a line of approximately equal length ; it is
hallowed by association with Shakespeare ; it is highly
flexible and appropriate for any sentiment. So the great
majority of translators have concurred in translating from
Greek into English iambics. Some, notably Murray, have
introduced rhyme. This is unnecessary and distracting.
In Murray's version of the *Electra* of Euripides, the Old
Man reports to Electra his findings at her father's grave :

> But now I turned aside
> To see my master's grave. All, far and wide,
> Was silence ; so I bent these knees of mine
> And wept and poured drink offerings from the wine
> I bear the strangers, and about the stone
> Laid myrtle sprays. And, child, I saw thereon
> Just at the censer slain, a fleeced ewe,
> Deep black, in sacrifice : the blood was new
> About it : and a tress of bright brown hair
> Shorn as in mourning close. Long stood I there
> And wondered, of all men what man had gone
> In mourning to that grave — My child, 'tis none
> In Argos. Did there come — Nay, mark me now. . .
> Thy brother in the dark, last night, to bow
> His head before that unadoréd tomb ?
> O come, and mark the colour of it. Come
> And lay thine own hair by that mourner's tress !
> A hundred little things make likenesses
> In brethren born, and shew the father's blood.

The value of this speech lies in the excitement of the revelation. The Old Man's recitation rises step by step to the climax of the last few lines ; it is Electra's brother, come home again! Murray's use of rhyme destroys this climax by imposing an arbitrary closure at the end of each couplet, reducing the mounting urgency of the Greek to one monotonous level. In addition, it is difficult to rhyme convincingly and still keep the original meaning. The necessity of rhyming assumes undue importance, making the translator begin at the end of his line and work backwards. (Note the weakness of some of the rhymes, particularly in the last complete couplet.) Milton's admonition is worth remembering :

The Measure is English Heroic Verse without Rime, as that of Homer in Greek, and of Virgil in Latin ; Rime being no necessary Adjunct or true Ornament of Poem or good

Verse, in longer works especially, but the Invention of a barbarous Age, to set off wretched matter and lame Meeter ; grac't indeed since by the use of some famous modern Poets, carried away by Custom, but much to their own vexation, hindrance and constraint to express many things otherwise, and for the most part worse then else they would have exprest them.

The iambic pentameter's one defect is its length. We have already remarked how it is often necessary for English to expand. If the translator restricts himself to the pentameter, line-for-line translation becomes impossible. In the Loeb series of translations, the books' layout — Greek text and translation on facing pages — while of great convenience to the reader, makes a rigid line-by-line translation inevitable. Thus at times the English is so tortuous as to be well-nigh incomprehensible. Here is a passage from Euripides' *Hippolytus* translated for Loeb by A. S. Way:

> Father, thy rage and strong-strained fury of soul
> Are fearful : yet, fair-seeming though the charge,
> If one unfold it, all unfair it is.
> I have no skill to speak before a throng ;
> My tongue is loosed with equals, and those few.
> And reason : they that are among the wise
> Of none account, to mobs are eloquent.

Some writers avoid this by using a longer line ; so Rex Warner in his *Medea* :

> Of all things which are living and can form a judgement
> We women are the most unfortunate creatures.
> Firstly, with an excess of wealth it is required
> For us to buy a husband and take for our bodies
> A master : for not to take one is even worse.
> And now the question is serious whether we take
> A good or bad one : for there is no easy escape
> For a woman, nor can she say no to her marriage.

But lines so long tend to become top-heavy ; for stage delivery, at any rate, they are unwieldy, and they offer a temptation to lapse into a colloquial style unsuited to tragedy. The line-by-line method is a useful challenge — every word counts, there is no room for loose writing or padding, and this will make the translation taut and interesting. But the translator should not be afraid of expanding to make the meaning clear — it is a necessary price for reconciling two languages so incompatible.

Metrical difficulties are greater in translating choruses. Lyric metres, as we have seen, were exceedingly complex. Greek, a highly polysyllabic language, can fit into many verse forms that sit upon English uneasily. Attempts have been made to reproduce the Greek structure in English, but these become no more than a jig-saw puzzle, with meaning and poetic values subordinate to metrical utility. This sort of word-juggling, a purely mechanical process, is admirable as a literary exercise ; it is the sort of thing one finds in the competition pages of more serious journals : but it cannot be said to advance the appreciation of the originals in any way. Some attempts have been felicitous. Rogers ingeniously translated Aristophanes into corresponding metres. Not only the metrical structure, but sometimes even the word-position, is reproduced in the English. Nor does this ingenuity ever grow tedious. Rogers' versions represent a consistently high level of literary achievement. Here is a chorus from his *Birds* about a coward who threw his shield away :

> We've been flying, we've been flying
> Over land and sea, espying
> Many a wonder strange and new.
> First, a tree of monstrous girth,

> Tall and stout, yet nothing worth,
> For 'tis rotten through and through ;
> It has got no heart, and we
> Heard it called 'Cleonymus-tree'.
> In the spring it blooms gigantic,
> Fig-traducing, sycophantic.
> Yet in falling leaf-time yields
> Nothing but a fall of shields.

Comedy, however, makes lighter demands on the translator. Rhyme is not out of place — indeed, pantomime rhymed couplets are highly appropriate. Nor does it matter so much if the rhymes are bad. But in the tragic chorus too close adherence to the original metre may choke all life out of the verse. It is safe to do as most translators have done and choose metres roughly equivalent but with longer lines, or indeed to use a different metre altogether. The author has experimented with trochaics (– ◡, the metre of *Hiawatha* and *Locksley Hall*) to replace the anapaests (◡ ◡ –) of the choruses of *Agamemnon*. English does not fit easily into anapaests but takes trochaics well.

It is dangerously easy for the translator who is a poet in his own right to impose his own style on the original to such an extent that the style of the Greek is lost. Pope's Homer is a conspicuous example. Nothing could be more alien to Homer than a passage like the following :

> Let Greece at length with pity touch thy breast,
> Thyself a Greek ; and, once, of Greeks the best !
> Lo ! every chief that might her fate prevent
> Lies pierced with wounds and bleeding in his tent.
> Eurypylus, Tydides, Atreus' son,
> And wise Ulysses, at the navy groan,
> More for their country's wounds than for their own.

We know we are reading Pope and not Homer ; the conscious art, precise rhyme and delicate balancing of clauses set the piece in a world far removed from the heroes of Homeric Troy. As a work of art it is none the worse for that. Taken in itself, it remains a fine poem. As a translation, it fails on many counts. The words of the original are there, but the spirit has gone.

The honest translator tries to reproduce the style of the original as faithfully as he can. In the case of Greek tragedy the difference between the authors is chronological as well as stylistic. Aeschylus' diction was considered old-fashioned by educated Greeks of the next generation. An accurate translator must recognize this and draw a sharp distinction between the language he uses for Aeschylus and for Euripides. J. E. Powell has recognized the problem in his translation of Herodotus, and indicated that writer's historical relationship to the corpus of Greek literature by translating into biblical English. Though at times self-conscious, this experiment is on the whole justified.

Thus it came to pass that Demaratus was put down from being king. And he fled from Sparta to the Medes because of an insult. After he was put down from being king, Demaratus was elected to rule as a magistrate. And at the feast of the Naked Boys, as Demaratus was watching the spectacle, Leotychides, that was now become king in his room, sent his servant and asked Demaratus in jest, to insult him, what it was like to be a magistrate after being a king. And he was angered by the question ; and he answered and said that he had now made trial of both, whereas Leotychides had not, but that his question should be the beginning of infinite good or infinite harm for Lacedaemon.

This catches the flavour of Herodotus' style far better than the modern idiom of Aubrey de Selincourt's version :

These were the events which led to the deposition of
Demaratus, but his leaving the country for Persia was the
result of an insulting remark which was later made to him
by Leotychides. After his deposition, Demaratus had been
elected to some other subordinate office in the state, and once,
when he was sitting amongst the spectators at the festival of
the Naked Boys, Leotychides, who was now king in his place,
sent his servant to ask him what it felt like to be a magistrate
after being a king. Hurt by the malicious question, the only
point of which was to jeer at him, Demaratus replied that,
though he himself had had experience of both offices, Leotychides had not. 'Nevertheless,' he added, 'this question will be
the beginning of great things for Sparta — either for good or
evil.'

Powell's defence of his method could apply with some
modifications to Aeschylus.

The language of the translation is, in the main, the English
of the Authorized version, though where it seemed necessary
I have replaced old by newer forms and used a small number
of words of later, though still of good, authority. I believe
that the simple and flowing language of Herodotus needs
least remoulding for modern English ears if presented in the
style and cadences rendered familiar by the Bible, and that a
certain quaintness and archaism thereby imparted make an
impression not dissimilar from that which the Ionic original
must have made upon Attic readers in the twenties of the
fifth century B.C.

However much we object to poetese, Aeschylus is probably
better served stylistically by a 'traditional' translation,
with its thees and thous, than by a more modern idiom.

Modernisms are likewise to be avoided in translations
from the other tragic poets. Euripides' 'modern' approach
to social problems has led some translators to produce racy

193

modern versions of his plays, but this falsifies his style. His diction was as far removed from everyday speech as that of Christopher Fry from the Englishman in the street. Tragic writing, like Virgil's Latin, was always consciously artificial. The modernizing tendency reaches its culmination in the translations of Ezra Pound. His version of Sophocles' *Philoctetes* is highly idiomatic and spiced with slang and jargon, an exciting play but with little relation to Sophocles. We find the same fault with Warner's *Prometheus*.

First then, you must turn away from here to the rising of the sun and go through lands that have not felt the plough. You will reach the roving Scythians who live raised up above the ground in wattle huts that rest upon the wheels of waggons. They are armed with long-range bows.

This deliberately pedestrian style lacks the grandeur of tragedy, and the 'long-range bows' strikes an incongruously modern note. (Compare Cecil Day Lewis's conscious modernisms in his Virgil translations — for example, 'municipal rackets'. These may jolt the reader into a new awareness, but are stylistically wrong.) But in an age when poetry draws its language from everyday life, it is difficult for the translator to avoid the twin pitfalls of poetese and jargon.

The problems in translating comedy are those of matter rather than of form and style. Comedy is more flexible in its use of metres. Aristophanes permits himself considerable freedom in this respect, so that a translation can jump from one metre to another, and from verse to prose, without violating the spirit of the original. Comedy takes its language from the vernacular and Greek slang can be paralleled by English. This means that comic translations date very quickly ; a version highly topical one year will be out of date the next, as nothing changes more quickly than slang. The best translations of past generations, like those of Rogers, now seem ponderous. Every generation needs a new translation of Aristophanes, while a good tragic version will retain its force for much longer.

The most inhibiting factor in translating Greek comedy is its material. Even in its most advanced literary form it retained the earthy humour of the original fertility rites. This was a natural form of humour to the Greeks, as it was to some extent to the Elizabethans. Modern moral consciousness, however, finds much of Aristophanes obscene, not only isolated and expurgable passages, but scenes vital to the plot (for example, the discovery of Mnesilochus dressed as a woman in *Thesmophoriazusae*, the latter half of *Peace*, and the whole of *Lysistrata*). Rogers, writing when condemnation of this form of humour was at its height, was sadly limited in his translations. For the *Thesmophoriazusae* he can only offer 'a free translation based on' Aristophanes, and parts of his *Lysistrata* are completely rewritten. To-day translators are allowed more freedom, though this varies in different times and countries ; Dudley Fitts' translation of *Lysistrata* was confiscated in the U.S.A. as obscene literature but licensed for public performance in this country with only half a dozen trifling excisions. The reader of Aristophanes in translation should bear in mind that he may not have the play in full, but its humour filtered through successive layers of scholarly reticence, conventional morality and public taste.

On matters of translation it is difficult to generalize ;

each combination of author and translator presents new problems, not least the generation in which the latter lives and the public for which he is writing. The following parallel examples from three plays show how the translator's ndividual bias may affect the work.

EURIPIDES — *CYCLOPS*

This play has been generally neglected by translators. Before A. S. Way's version for the Loeb series, the second piece quoted here, only two versions existed in English. The following is a chorus from Shelley's translation, made in 1819.

> For your gaping gulf and your gullet wide
> The ravin is ready on every side.
> The limbs of the strangers are cooked and done ;
> There is boiled meat and roast meat and meat
>   from the coal.
> You may chop it and tear it and gnash it for fun ;
> An hairy goat's skin contains the whole.
> Let me but escape and ferry me o'er
> The stream of your wrath to a safer shore.
>
> The Cyclops Aetnaean is cruel and bold.
> He murders the stranger
> That sits on his hearth,
> And dreads no avenger
> To rise from the earth.
>
> He roasts the men before they are cold ;
> He snatches them boiling from the coal
> And from the cauldron pulls them whole
> And minces their flesh and gnaws their bone
> With his cursèd teeth till all be gone.

Farewell, foul pavilion!
Farewell, rites of dread!
The Cyclops vermilion
With slaughter uncloying
Now feasts on the dead
In the flesh of strangers joying!

In this chorus we see the extent to which a poet can
impose his individual style and the literary mannerisms of
his time on the work of another age. This is not always
detrimental ; as we have seen, Pope's Homer, though
more Pope than Homer, is still a fine poem. But here the
union produces a hybrid belonging to neither age and
with no style of its own. Euripides was not squeamish.
Nor, we may assume, was his audience ; ancient taste
accepted much that jars on the more tender susceptibilities
of moderns. He delighted in bloodthirsty description, in
shocking by piling on horror. This chorus reflects the
tone of the whole play. It is difficult to imagine a cultural
ethos more unsympathetic to these qualities than the
Romantic movement. Shelley, though drawing much of
his inspiration from classical standards and ideals, saw the
Greek world through rose-coloured glasses. His conception of the golden age of Greece as pastoral, pure and
picturesque is as valid as a reconstruction of eighteenth-
century France entirely in terms of Le Petit Trianon. In
this version Euripides' full-bloodedness, his frank brutality,
are watered down with the stock Romantic vocabulary.
Shelley betrays himself early in the play by calling the
Cyclops' cave a 'grotto' ; we think of formal gardens
and picturesque follies when we should be thinking of a
sea-beaten cave on the shore, littered with the bony relics
of cannibal feasts. So here the cave becomes a 'pavilion' ;
apart from necessitating a dreadful rhyme, this word

evokes all the wrong associations. In itself, the chorus is not unpleasing ; it reads well, but the inconsistency between form and content makes it negligible as translation.

Way's version (1912) makes a more serious attempt to come to terms with the spirit of the play.

> Gape wide your jaws, you one-eyed beast,
> Your tiger-fangs, an' a' that ;
> Hot from the coals to make your feast.
> Here's roast, an' boiled, an' a' that.
> For a' that, an' a' that.
> His guid fur-rug an' a' that,
> He's tearin', champin' flesh o' guests !
> So nane for me, for a' that.
>
> Ay, paddle your ain canoe, One-eye,
> Wi' bluidy oars, an' a' that :
> Your impious hall, I pass it by !
> I cry 'avaunt !' for a' that.
> For a' that, an' a' that.
> Your 'Etna Halls' an' a' that.
> Your joy in gorgin' strangers' flesh !
> Awa' wi' ye, for a' that.
>
> A heartless wretch is he, whoe'er,
> When shipwrecked men, an' a' that,
> Draw nigh his hearth wi' suppliant prayer,
> Slays, eats them up, an' a' that.
> For a' that, an' a' that.
> His stews and steaks, an' a' that.
> His teeth are foul wi' flesh o' man !
> He's damned to hell, for a' that !

Way here employs a device frequently used by translators of comedy. He takes the form of a well-known modern poem and adapts Euripides' words to fit it. This can be highly successful. Patric Dickinson, in his version of the *Acharnians* of Aristophanes, translates a fertility song into calypso rhythm, and the result is exactly right. Way's use of Scottish songs as models for the *Cyclops* choruses is less successful. His choice of Burns here seems purely arbitrary. It is common practice to translate into Scots when the Greek is written in dialect — again, this can be done in the *Acharnians* in the scene with the Boeotian, who enters to the skirling of bagpipes. But there is no justification for using dialect here. The choruses are written in as pure Attic as the rest of the play. As in Shelley's version, the brutality of the original is lost. What was savage in Greek becomes harmless jollity in translation, lapsing at times, particularly in the first stanza, into incomprehensibility. Yet the experiment is not altogether unsuccessful. At least we have the impression that the chorus is meant to be sung, and sung with a swing, something of which we have no hint in Shelley (for another chorus Way uses *The Keel Row* as a model, which brings out this quality even more strongly). Way is hearty where Shelley is limp, forceful where Shelley is merely pretty. Way's version would certainly come out more strongly on the stage, though dialect weakens the effect. Neither is faithful to the original, either in content or in tone, but Way's translation comes far nearer to catching the spirit of this earthy play.

AESCHYLUS — *PROMETHEUS BOUND*

A great cry has risen from the world's compassion ;
   The peoples of the sunset, they go grieving by the sea
For a beauty long ago, for a greatness of old fashion.
   Thine and thy brethren's, in the days when ye were free.
In the Lords of Holy Asia there is wakened a strange passion,
   And the lips of them that perish pine for thee.

> Yea, the Amazons, the dwellers beyond Phasis,
>   Who love not, who battle without fear ;
> And the hordes that wander in fierce places
>   At the world's rim, the Scythians of the Mere ;
> And hard men, of Araby the flower,
>   Where the high crags of Caucasus advance,
> They groan in their mountain-builded tower,
>   Amid great wrath and flashing of the lance.

This is part of the chorus in which the Oceanids lament the fate of Prometheus ; the translation is by Gilbert Murray. Murray's translations have done more than the work of any other writer to bring Greek drama to the general public. He translated most of the extant plays and all the greatest ; his last, Aristophanes' *Knights*, was published a year before his death. He is generally at his happiest in comedy, where he shows a fine sense of rhythm — his choruses from the *Frogs* go with a great swing — and of fun. His insistence on rhyme, however, sometimes leads him to perpetrate strange errors of judgement ; his *Frogs* contains the couplet

> I put things on the stage that came from daily life and
>   business
> When men could catch me if I tripped, could listen without
>   dizziness.

But such things may be overlooked in the overriding good humour of his versions. In tragedy his great weakness is his love of archaisms. There are several in the passage quoted above — the use of ye, thee, yea ; 'mere' for 'lake' ; 'mountain-builded'. As we have seen, this is not inappropriate in Aeschylus. It gives a sense of period, and, consciously or not, sets the author in the correct historical perspective. When Murray applies the same technique to Euripides the results are less pleasing. Many of his archaisms are unnecessary ; one has the impression that he went out of his way to use older word-forms where modern would have done as well or better. The following passages, from Euripides' *Electra* and *Rhesus* respectively, show his style at its most extravagant.

> Would God that He had made thee clean of soul!
> Helen and thou — O, face and form were fair,
> Meet for man's praise ; but sisters twain ye were,
> Both things of naught, a stain on Castor's star.

> Back, back, ye twain! Are ye in love with death ?
> Laertes' son, thy sword into the sheath!
> Our golden Thracian gaspeth in his blood ;
> The steeds are ours ; the foe hath understood
> And crowds against you. Haste ye! haste to fly, —
> Ere yet the lightning falleth, and ye die!

In Aeschylus, however, Murray's supremacy is generally acknowledged. His version of the Prometheus chorus does not lack grandeur ; the fine words and phrases roll off the tongue like Aeschylus' Greek, and there is a real sense of poetry. He is never so entirely at his ease with later writers.

The following version by Rex Warner, a writer who is not a professional scholar, was published in 1947.

> Now the whole earth has raised a cry of mourning.
> All men lament the dying out of the splendid
> time-honoured noble fame
> of yours and of your brothers.
> All mortals dwelling in
> houses and homes of holy Asia
> in your hard grievous suffering
> weep and lament with you.
> and the maidens who are fearless in the fight,

> they who dwell in Kolchis' land,
> and the hordes who are in Scythia, and there
> at the furthest point of earth
> live around Maeotis' lake.
>
> and the battle honoured flower of Asia,
> men who hold by Caucasus
> their precipitous and rocky citadel,
> savage armies roaring out
> in the biting of the blade.

This is the antithesis of Murray. Warner describes his methods in his introduction to *Medea*.

Without doubt some translations are better than others, and, if the purpose of a translation is to convey something of the spirit of the original to those who are ignorant of the original language, then I think that the laborious trans-literators are more to be commended than the brilliant dis-tortionists . . . it seems far safer to stick as closely as possible to the original. Indeed, even those who are poets themselves have rightly adopted this method. Browning, for instance, translates almost word for word and, to my mind, is the more admirable for that, in spite of his rigidities and obscurities.

The great virtue of this method is clarity ; Warner's version is eminently readable, and contains nothing to give anyone a moment's pause. Its dramatic quality is another matter. Its failing is its flatness. Where Murray's lines roll magnificently, Warner's inevitably tend towards the prosaic, which Aeschylus never was. (For this reason Warner's laconic and textureless style is more successful with Euripides.) Nevertheless, Warner does himself an injustice in calling himself a 'laborious transliterator'. His 'biting of the blade' is a keener image than Murray's 'flashing of the lance'. His style is more trenchant through its simplicity ; not a word is wasted, and his verse has more immediate impact than Murray's. But what it gains in clarity it loses in warmth, and there is nothing clinical about Aeschylus.

SOPHOCLES — *PHILOCTETES*

PHILOCTETES. O strangers!
Who may ye be, and from what country have ye put into this land, that is harbourless and desolate ? What should I deem to be your city or your race ? The fashion of your garb is Greek — most welcome to my sight, — but I fain would hear your speech ; and do not shrink from me in fear, or be scared by my wild looks ; nay, in pity for one wretched and lonely, for a sufferer so desolate and so friendless, speak to me, if indeed ye have come as friends, — Oh, answer ! 'Tis not meet that I should fail of this, at least, from you, or ye from me.
NEOPTOLEMUS. Then know this first, good sir, that we are Greeks — since thou art fain to learn that.
PHILOCTETES. O well-loved sound ! Ah, that I should indeed be greeted by such a man, after so long a time ! What quest, my son, hath drawn thee towards these shores, and to this spot ? What enterprise ? What kindliest of winds ? Speak, tell me all, that I may know what thou art.

This translation was made by Richard Jebb, Regius Professor of Greek at Cambridge, and published in 1898. It is included here as an example of what the general reader should avoid, though not from any fault of the translator's. The primary function of translation is, after all, to convey meaning. When all education was grounded in the classics, those interested in the plays as literature read them in the original ; there was no equivalent of the educated but non-Greek-reading public of to-day. Thus there was no need for a literary translation reproducing as far as possible the style and nuances of the original ; translation's function was to elucidate the text. This is the purpose of Jebb's version. Style and dramatic content are sacrificed to meaning. The translation is almost literal ; the order of the Greek clauses, the smallest particles are carefully reproduced, where a 'literary' translator would invert, rearrange or omit. (Compare the history of Bible translation ; the earliest translations, first into Latin and then into English, concentrated exclusively on meaning ; only later could the work be given a pleasing literary style.) It is a painstaking and meticulous translation, bearing as much relation to the original as a stuffed bird to the living creature.

> PHILOCTETES. Ahoy there !
>> Men, who are you ? What country is it you come from
>> To this strange coast ? There is no harbour here,
>> No home for any man. . . . What blood ? What city ?
>> I cannot guess. Greeks surely, though, I'd say,
>> By the look of your clothes — and God be thanked for
>>> that.
>> If I could hear your language. . . . Have no fear !
>> You're scared at my looks, more like a savage creature
>> Than a man. But have no fear ; pity me rather.
>> I am a poor lonely creature, a castaway
>> Without a friend in the world, much wronged. . . .
>> Speak, men !
> NEOPTOLEMUS. My friend,
>> We are Greeks. That question can be answered first.
> PHILOCTETES. O lovely sound ! After so many years
>> To hear that greeting ! O my lad, my son,
>> What brings you here ? What errand ? What blessed
>>> wind ?
>> Who are you ? Tell me. Let me hear you speak.

Nothing could be further from Jebb's purpose and approach than this version by E. F. Watling (1953). Jebb was a scholar writing for scholars. Watling writes for the general public. His translation is naturalistic, and clearly written with the metre in mind; the opening 'Ahoy there!' sets the tone of the scene. Though he uses verse form, Watling lapses into prose for the longer speeches, and his verse is simple, using normal conversational English, never obtrusive. The virtues and vices of this method have been touched on already in this chapter. Watling avoids the more serious pitfalls, but his translation still lacks dignity. In Greek tragedy there is little distinction of style between characters. Philoctetes the savage castaway uses the same lofty diction as Oedipus the king. Thus Watling's naturalism strikes a false note, the whining tone of

> I am a poor lonely creature, a castaway
> Without a friend in the world . . .

though appropriate to the modern conception of a man in such circumstance, is not the language of Sophocles' tragic hero. This passage also shows how the conversational may lapse into the banal. Nevertheless Watling's version probably represents the best that can be done in bringing Greek tragedy to a popular audience. His highly contemporary dialogue brings out the eternal contemporaneity of the themes.

These examples have only been quoted to show that no translation is perfect. (The reader may care to amuse himself by criticizing the author's own translations used throughout this book.) It is easy to carp, but in each there is much to admire. Let the reader only bear in mind that the translator may be influenced by circumstances quite external to the work he is translating; by his public, the form in which he works, the cultural background of his time, even the typographical arrangement of his pages ; and a reading of several translations will offset many of these difficulties. To recommend individual translations is invidious, but a complete list would certainly include The Loeb Classical Library series, if only for its completeness — many plays have not been translated elsewhere ; for Aeschylus, Headlam, Murray, Warner ; for Sophocles, Sheppard, FitzGerald ; for Euripides, Warner again and Vellacott ; for Aristophanes, Rogers and Fitts. Lucas's *Greek Drama for Everyman* gives several complete translations and many selected passages, while the Penguin Classics series is always interesting and eminently actable.

CHAPTER XI

ANCIENT AND MODERN

A LL over Greece, and on the coast of Asia Minor and in Sicily where once the great Greek colonies flourished, may be found ruins of ancient theatres, a happy hunting-ground for historian and archaeologist. Besides the important centres, Athens, Corinth, Epidauros, Delphi, Delos, there are the remains of many small theatres built for local festivities. These are especially plentiful in the country round Athens — Oropus and Thoricos, for example, and the Piraeus. Some of them, auditorium and all, could almost fit comfortably into the orchestra at Athens. They all followed the same basic pattern, though each was modified to suit local needs and conditions. At Thoricos, as we have seen, the rock formation made a rectangular orchestra easier to build than the normal round one. At Corinth the natural rise and fall of the ground was utilized in setting out the *skene*, which may have been displaced to one side instead of keeping the normal symmetrical arrangement. At Oropus the theatre was hollowed out of a hillside, which backed on to a row of shops, and had to be approached by a steep flight of steps. Natural ditches and rock fissures were used for drainage, and the chorus was forced to descend into the orchestra down steep ramps. At Pergamon in Asia Minor the theatre cut across the passage to the temple, and so the *skene* was made removable. When the theatre was needed, a temporary structure was erected on posts let into the ground. At Megalopolis the stage was portable and kept in a large shed. So in every place local craftsmen constructed, in their own fashion and the materials at hand, their living shrines to Dionysus.

Time has dwelt harshly with many of these theatres. Changing needs caused shifts of population. Cities which, in an agricultural economy had been thriving centres of art and commerce, were deserted. The modern city of Corinth is several miles from its ancient namesake, and at Oropus the shrine of the hero Amphiaraus with its tiny theatre has only one cottage marking what was once a crowded street. As the greatness of Greek drama declined the theatres were put to increasingly ignoble uses. We have seen how the orchestra of the Theatre of Dionysus at Athens was flooded for mimic sea-battles to gratify the coarser tastes of a later age. A chronicler records as the ultimate degradation that it was used for puppet-shows. It now presents a sorry spectacle. In the auditorium the upper tiers have vanished. At orchestra level the foundations of the *skene* alone remain, with part of the Roman stage, a complicated accretion of the work of centuries. The orchestra itself, where once Aeschylus' mighty choruses were heard, is now inhabited by lizards, tourists and photographers. The site has been carefully railed off and preserved as an ancient monument, but nothing has been done to renovate it or restore it to use.

So in almost every case the ancient theatres have crumbled away. Overlaid with Roman additions, their fabric plundered at random for other buildings, exposed to the wear and tear of time, they are but skeletons of their former selves. In some places the villagers do not even know what they are. For centuries no attempt was made to study or record them before it was too late. Tourists with an historical bent made sentimental pilgrimages to the sites, but without knowledge or appreciation. A typical account appears in the *Annual Register* for 1760, under the title, 'A description of the first theatre that was ever built, called the Theatre of Bacchus at Athens'.

As to (the place) which was designed for the actors . . . the orchestra was about four feet from the ground ; its figure was an oblong square, thirty-six feet in length, extending from the stage to the rows of benches ; its breadth is not mentioned in the memoirs I have of the dimensions of this theatre, which were taken on the spot about one hundred years since by M. de la Guillatière an ingenious traveller. In certain places of it the music, the chorus and the mimics were conveniently disposed. Among the Romans it was put to a more honourable use, for the Emperor and Senate had places upon it. Upon the flat of the orchestra, towards the place of the actors, was an elevation, or platform, called logeon, or thymele, which among the Romans was called pulpitum : it was higher than the orchestra ; its figure was square, being six feet on every side ; and in this place the principal part of the chorus made their recitation, and in the comical interludes the mimics used to perform on it.

Scholars of to-day, when every stone in the theatre has been measured and debated, might perhaps envy the age when such sweeping and erratic generalizations could pass unchallenged.

It is only recently that the theatres have been seriously studied. Archaeology as a science began in the nineteenth century. Before this, explorations were haphazard, the work of cultured dilettantes more interested in finding some quaint antique to decorate a nobleman's house than in making a contribution to knowledge. Since then, the sites have been properly examined, surveyed, photographed and recorded for posterity. It has been realized that even the smallest theatre may teach us as much as that of Athens itself. Much has been learnt and most of the important remains excavated, but much remains to be done in the way of interpretation.

Some theatres have escaped the ravages of time and are still used for their original purposes. One of these is the Theatre of Epidauros. This was more fortunate than others in avoiding Roman alterations, being allowed, for example, to retain its circular orchestra intact. Perhaps the peculiar sanctity of the site, shrine of Asklepios, God of Healing, protected it, for the Romans built their own *odeum* (music-hall) some distance away. Thus it is the best preserved example of theatre-building now extant. Though built after the greatest period of the drama, at the beginning of the fourth century B.C., it embodies all the classical features. Archaeologists have restored the foundations of the stone *skene* to their conjectural position and replaced the great double gateway over one *parodos*.

Epidauros itself, with the ruins of its houses, temples and monuments, is now deserted. Only a museum stands on the site. The nearest town is Nauplion, a drive of ninety minutes, on the edge of the Gulf of Argos. Despite these disadvantages, it was decided to use the theatre for a festival of ancient tragedy. The stone auditorium was refaced and made safe, and under the direction of scholars a temporary wooden *skene* and platform erected at the edge of the orchestra. Ancient conditions of acting, setting and production were reproduced as far as possible. There were a few concessions to modern techniques. As it was necessary to perform at night, the full resources of modern stage lighting were called in. Sometimes, too, the action extended beyond the confines of the stage to the adjoining slopes of the hill, where gods and goddesses appeared among the trees. Actors were for the most part confined to the stage and the chorus to the orchestra, though mingling when necessary ; in Euripides' *Hippolytus* the procession bore the hero's body reverently into the centre of the orchestra, and Theseus left the stage to come down and weep over his son.

Another ancient theatre still brought regularly to life is also post-classical, of far later construction. It is the Theatre of Herodes Atticus in Athens, named after its creator, a wealthy Greek scholar and patron of the arts of the second century A.D. His name is associated with many monuments to culture and learning, of which this theatre was among the finest. Situated on the slope of the Acropolis, it is barely more than a stone's throw from its earlier counterpart, the Theatre of Dionysus. It is Roman in design, with a semicircular orchestra. The original fabric has suffered with time, though most of the elaborately arched *skene* still remains intact to form an impressive background to the presentations. Stage and seating have been carefully restored. The tiered seats stretch most of the way up the hillside, and above that the spectators accommodate themselves as best they can on the bare rock. The excellence of the acoustics has already been remarked upon. In size the theatre is particularly impressive. Its vast stage can hold a cast of over two hundred. This makes it peculiarly suitable for opera, where large choruses can be deployed to full advantage. Symphony concerts are also given in the orchestra.

Each summer the theatre is used for productions of ancient tragedies. These are eagerly awaited, and attract large audiences from the city. First nights are gala occasions, and the police are out in force to marshal the crowds filling the road to the theatre as they did in days gone by. For tragic performances the size of the stage is considerably reduced, both by permanent scenic units which reproduce the entrances of the ancient theatre and by cunning lighting, which illuminates only the centre of the stage and leaves the rest in darkness. As at Epidauros modern lighting techniques are used to full advantage. The orchestra, a pool of blackness, slowly fills with light as the chorus enter and returns to darkness again as they leave. The chorus movements are directed with great beauty and skill. Now advancing on the audience, now retreating, now crossing the orchestra in a diagonal pattern, now draping themselves frieze-like along the front of the stage, they maintain an unbroken formal unity against which the action proceeds. Their movements echo and emphasize the emotions expressed on the stage. They cower at moments of fear, raise their arms aloft in triumph, swirl apart and come together in excitement. The chorus is used not only to deliver its own part but as a constant balletic accompaniment to the actors.

Some concessions have to be made to the modern public. The plays are given either in modern Greek translations or in the ancient text with modern pronunciation. Either way the value of the complicated metre is lost. as modern Greek pronunciation depends on stress, not, as formerly, on length of syllables. Also, the actors go unmasked — a pity, as from the upper tiers of the auditorium faces are blurred, and masks would help. (Modern works performed in this ancient setting offer striking illustrations of the difficulties the Greek actor had to cope with — in opera, for example, it is almost impossible to see which one of a group of soloists is singing, so great is the distance between them and the audience.) Nevertheless these productions are probably as close to the ancient

spirit as the modern commercial theatre can go. It is a moving experience to sit on the hillside under the evening sky, watching the audience assemble and the guests of honour processing across the orchestra to their seats in the front row as they did when the plays were first performed. The new techniques, too, may sometimes produce unexpected effects. The combination of artificial light and open air had a macabre result in Euripides' *Hecuba*, where the ghost of Polydorus laments outside his mother's tent. The ghostly effect was enhanced by numbers of bats, attracted by the spotlights, wheeling and squeaking above the stage. It was an effect that would have delighted Euripides.

Even the smaller theatres have their moments of glory.

Touring groups like the Greek Ancient Drama Company give summer performances in various provincial towns. Groups from other countries also make occasional visits. These are mostly amateurs, whose enthusiasm sometimes exceeds their talent, but there is a real attempt to keep the splendour of the ancient drama alive and present the plays in the settings for which they were intended.

Athens is well provided with theatres of all kinds, but, apart from the special performances described above, the ancient drama is unaccountably neglected. Greece has been subjected to so many influences in the course of a long and chequered history that newer traditions have eradicated the old. When the classical drama died, the Greek theatre entered its own dark age. Christianity brought no reviving influence — there is no great body of biblically inspired drama, as in our own country. Sundry passages exist — a dialogue, for example, between Adam, Eve and the Serpent in dramatic form — but these were almost certainly not intended for the stage. Fragments of old heroic sagas found their way into mediaeval literature in more or less garbled forms, but had no real hand in its shaping. Greece forgot its classical drama as it forgot so many of its ancient glories, and formed its theatre from other elements. So there are two main streams in the modern Greek theatre. Translations of foreign classics are popular, and plays considered dated here may still be topical in Greece. Wilde's *Lady Windermere's Fan* is performed as a modern problem play in a country where the treatment of women is archaic by Western standards and divorce carries considerable social stigma. The second stream is mainly pastoral, plays based on country and village life and calling on the colourful folk-lore of various districts, where local dances and traditions are still preserved. These plays are often simple and unsophisticated in dramatic content, though lending themselves to vivid production.

A typical example is *The Shepherd's Lover*. In the open-air theatre a whole village street has been set up — a row of houses with practicable windows and balconies in the background, a real bridge, and a fountain playing merrily on the fore-stage. A spotlight picks out an old shepherd sitting idly on a rock. He acts as narrator and chorus, introducing the story and characters to the audience and pausing now and then to play his pipe. A rich and gallant chieftain, Mitros, has searched all Greece for the pretty shepherdess he had loved twenty years before, but of whom he has since lost all trace. Arriving at the village, he sits down by the fountain to rest. The village girls cross the bridge and come down to the fountain for water, iugs on their heads, accompanying their labours with a haunting folk-song. One of them, Croustallo, reminds Mitros strongly of his lost love. When the others go he holds her in conversation and gives her a gold cross and chain. Croustallo's mother Maro, the prettiest widow in the village, is naturally anxious that her daughter should marry this handsome stranger who gives such rich presents, instead of Liakos, the poor shepherd boy to whom she is betrothed. But as soon as Maro meets Mitros she recognizes him as her long-lost lover. In a scene of high melodrama, with plentiful asides to the audience, she decides not to reveal herself for fear he will think her old and ugly. Mitros, however, refuses to marry Croustallo. He is still hoping to find his past love. Maro, determined to bring the match about, lies to him. She says that she knew the girl in question, who died in her arms many years before. The disclosure has the opposite effect to what she intended. Mitros, far from reconciling himself to marrying her daughter, determines to renounce the world and become a monk. Such scenes are dear to the hearts of the Greek audience. Mitros' passionate speech is cheered to the echo.

He is prevented by the intervention of Liakos, Croustallo's betrothed. Anxious above all for Croustallo's happiness, he quarrels with Mitros. They fight ; the audience gasp as he flies at him with a knife. Liakos insists that he marry her. He reluctantly agrees, and the wedding preparations go forward. The villagers appear and celebrate the betrothal in another colourful dance. Into this scene of merriment breaks a gloomy figure, Liakos' mother. Furious at what she considers a slight on her son, she lays a curse on the marriage. The scene between the two mothers is played with all the melo-dramatic stops full out. Liakos' mother curses with all the vigour of a tragedy queen while Maro cowers at the other side of the stage. Afraid that the old woman's hatred will harm her daughter, Maro realizes that the only way to stop the marriage is to reveal her secret. This she does by singing, inside her house, an old song which she and her lover sang together as children. Mitros, standing outside, hears it and is amazed ; then Maro emerges and all is made known.

Having found his true love, he gladly yields Croustallo to Liakos. All ends happily in the celebration of the two marriages. Typically the play closes with a long scene of dance and festivity as the procession of villagers, carrying the wedding wreaths aloft on high poles, move across the bridge to a gay rhythm and disappear once more into their houses as the lights go down.

This simple and unvarnished tale loses much in summary. The plot resembles those of our own Victorian theatre — thwarted lovers, concealed identity, quarrels and a duel, a curse, discovery by means of a song, a happy ending. It might be the libretto for a Verdi opera. Yet in performance the play is rich in action and good humour. It is full of those strong dramatic scenes loved by the Greeks, and punctuated by applause at stirring speeches or moving episodes. In the large cast every villager is an individual, and the whole is enlivened by colourful local costumes, song and dances. It is a typical example of an important school of native drama, but one would look in vain for the influence of Aeschylus or Sophocles. There is something Aristophanic in the characterization of the villagers — the fat pompous elders, the old shepherds, the dwarf — but there is nothing beyond this remotely resembling the drama of antiquity. In England we can trace the development of the drama without a break from its origins in the mediaeval church to the present day. There were foreign influences in plenty, but all were embodied in the national pattern and made no radical changes. In Greece the perfected art-forms of the classical age were abandoned, and superseded after many years by the folk-art of a new culture and a new way of life.

Modern styles of acting and production are the complete antithesis of the ancient. Flamboyance has replaced simplicity. Producers are fond of crowd scenes in which everyone does something different, kaleidoscopic effects of whirling colour to appeal to the eye. This is evident not only in their own plays but in productions of foreign works sometimes ill-suited to the Greek love of display. Acting is bold and forceful. Greek actors are not ashamed of over-emphasis or unashamedly theatrical declamation. Their performances combine the frank enjoyment of children's make-believe with the skill and physical discipline of ballet.

Western critics would denounce this style as 'ham', but it is a welcome antidote to the wink-and-whisper school predominant in our own theatre. Greek actors trying to imitate Western styles are forced and artificial. The actor playing Hamlet in the production mentioned earlier was taken severely to task by critics and public for allowing his conception to be influenced by Olivier's film. In stamina alone the modern actor resembles his predecessors. To perform for a whole morning in the three plays of a trilogy, playing a variety of parts with only brief intervals, was no mean feat. Two performances of *Hamlet* were given in immediate succession. Hamlet had no sooner died in Horatio's arms than he had to reappear on the castle walls with his father's ghost. The Greek theatre of to-day is strong, exuberant and alive, but its strength springs from a later culture, and owes nothing to the severe discipline and calculated economy of effect that marked the ancient drama in its greatest period.

So to our own country. To what extent have these masterpieces been played on our stage? We must answer, to our shame, very little. Roman comedy was performed in mediaeval times, but of Greek drama there was little or nothing. The great actors of past centuries were blind to its possibilities. There is no record of Kean as Orestes or of Mrs. Siddons terrifying her audience as Clytemnestra.

The full-blooded acting of the period, with its love of emotional effects and rhodomontade, may have found the Greek restraint inimical. Irving played Jason in *Medea* at Birmingham in 1856, though this was probably not Euripides' version.

Things had come to such a pass that when Martin-Harvey wished to present himself as Oedipus in 1912, the best available version was still Dryden's. He then considered commissioning a new play which would combine Sophocles' story with explanatory scenes showing Oedipus' life before he came to rule in Thebes, but found the Lord Chamberlain unwilling to license a play on such a subject. To such an extent had the Greek drama been forgotten.

Eventually the controversial director Max Reinhardt was brought over from Germany to produce Martin-Harvey in Sophocles' play. Reinhardt had achieved notoriety on the Continent for his unconventional approach to problems of staging. He came near to Greek methods in bringing actor and audience into contact by abolishing the barrier of the proscenium stage. The spectator found himself at the heart of a tremendous spectacle. This production aroused widespread public interest and was the first serious attempt for many years to bring Greek tragedy to a modern audience. The following is a contemporary account.

As at Berlin and Frankfurt, the whole of the interior of the theatre was made to serve the 'scene' ; the entire proscenium was fitted with a black screen representing the front of the palace of Oedipus. The centre of this screen was occupied by high, impressive brass doors, on either side of which were three massive black columns supporting a grim portico, with a piece projecting from the centre on which the altar was placed. On either side of this 'apron' flights of steps led to the arena, or ball-floor of the theatre. This floor formed a lower stage, and was built up in order to enable the spectator to realize that he was participating in the scene before him. In pursuit of the intimacy idea, space was cleared in front of the stage by removing rows of stalls, for the chorus and crowd to act in and mix with the spectators. The front row of the stalls was, in fact, in touch with the outer fringe of the crowd, while all the players made their entrances and exits through the audience at various points in the arena.

The scene was lit from all points of the theatre according to the new methods, whereby coloured limes are thrown on neutral surfaces and the desired effects obtained by mixing the coloured rays as they fall upon each object. The principal aim of the lighting was, however, to keep a blinding white light beating upon the palace and to break it up with vivid bits of colour. The general conception of colour black and white, great masses of white, sometimes tinted with yellow, moving against the dense blue background which occasionally deepened to violet.

Perhaps the most artistic effect was that attained by the crowd and Oedipus. Oedipus stood on the rostrum calm and self-possessed. Beneath him surged the infuriated mob, with outstretched arms, swelling up to him like a sea of angry emotions, and returning thence to the Leader of the Chorus in response to his call. There on one side Oedipus stood like an intellectual pinnacle islanded in the billowing ocean of human beings ; and there on the other side the Leader stood like the Spirit of the Infinite, swayed to and fro by elemental passions.

Of this exciting spectacle one can only say that it was magnificent, but it was not Sophocles. Yet it had the effect, however temporary, of impressing on the theatre-going public that there might be something in Greek tragedy after all.   Professor Kitto saw the same results with *Antigone* :

It was produced (Harrower's translation) in a large circus ; the ring became the orchestra, and a narrow stage was erected at the back.   Two choruses were used, one to dance, the other placed on either side of the stage to sing.   It ran for a week ; on the first two nights the audience was all high-brow and paper, on the last two the populace was fighting to get in.

On the whole, however, managements think Greek drama a bad risk.   They believe, perhaps rightly, that the public will fight shy of plays not only written so long ago, but dealing with themes beside which the matter of most contemporary drama pales into insignificance.   The dismal record of public taste over the years justifies their reluctance, though a controversial director like Reinhardt or the appearance of a well-known actor may arouse occasional interest.   An actor wanting a great star part will find one ready-made in most Greek tragedies.   A few have balanced their personal popularity and box-office appeal against the unfamiliarity of the plays — Olivier in *Oedipus Rex*, Wolfit in that play and *Oedipus at Colonus* presented as one programme, Sybil Thorndike in *The Trojan Women*, Eileen Herlie in *Medea*.   Sometimes a management with high artistic standards and an assured audience will venture on the lesser-known plays.   Sir Barry Jackson, as well as sponsoring Bernard Shaw, introduced Murray's translations to the public.   Yet these remain but isolated instances. Of ancient comedy the commercial theatre has nothing to offer save for occasional revivals of *Lysistrata,* whose sex-motif and reputation for indecency can always be relied on to attract an audience.

Radio has been more adventurous.   It has much to

commend it as a medium for Greek plays. The audience is forced to rely on its imagination to construct the setting ; the poetry can come over without distraction. Memorable performances have been given of MacNeice's translation of *Agamemnon*, Murray's and Fitts' *Frogs*, Dickinson's *Acharnians* and *Peace*, Vellacott's *Helen*, and many others.

On the stage Greek drama has been mainly left to the amateurs. In schools and universities a living classical tradition and an assured, knowledgeable audience provide an ideal atmosphere for producing the plays. When at the end of the last century Oxford amateurs were petitioning the University authorities for permission to form their own dramatic society, unexpected support came from Dr. Jowett, then Master of Balliol. He had the revolutionary idea that it might be an aid to study to see the Greek plays in performance. Largely through his influence the O.U.D.S. was formed and found a theatre, and a clause inserted in the constitution that every three years a Greek play should be given in the original. Unfortunately the Society failed to keep its promise. In recent years the only tragedy produced has been *Hippolytus* in translation.

Individual colleges have made greater contributions, notably and appropriately Balliol. For some years the Balliol Players have carried on a lively experiment in taking Aristophanes to the schools and general public. Each summer one comedy is taken on tour. Humour is brought up to date by using modern translations and replacing ancient by modern topicalities. Large parts of the plot which may be difficult for a modern audience to understand are completely rewritten. Costume is a mixture of ancient and modern. **In a recent production of the *Clouds***

Socrates wore a frock coat and bowler hat, while the chorus unashamedly combined Greek draperies with spectacles. In the debate between True and False Reasoning on the merits of hot baths, True Reasoning (the cold-bath advocate) was dressed as a Scoutmaster. With so many modifications the productions tend to be entertainments on Aristophanic themes rather than what the author actually wrote, but convey the spirit and guiding principles of Greek comedy with great success.

At Cambridge a Greek play is performed in the original every three years with a cast of University actors and actresses. Within the limits of the proscenium stage these are excellent of their kind, though often scenically over-elaborate. Modern box-stage theatres are unfriendly to Greek drama, and the various devices resorted to, such as bringing the chorus along the front of the auditorium, are unconvincing and little help. Great attention is paid to choral speaking, and special music composed for the productions. Vaughan Williams' popular *Wasps* overture was written for a Cambridge performance, and Stanford composed music for the *Frogs*. Cambridge has indulged in its own experiments in bringing Aristophanes up to date — the *Frogs* with choruses set to Noel Coward tunes, and the *Birds* produced in the early 'thirties introducing, among other topical personalities, Mussolini.

Another centre of pilgrimage for lovers of Greek drama is Bradfield College, in Berkshire. Here the difficulties of indoor production have been obviated by the construction of a small Greek theatre in the College grounds, reproducing as faithfully as possible all the conditions of the original. Max Beerbohm has exquisitely evoked the atmosphere of a Bradfield performance.

It is an exact replica of a real Attic theatre, and in the midst of its round orchestra stands a little white altar, green-garlanded, inscribed with the legend 'Dionysus'. Thereon burns a flame, pale under the sunlight of an English June. From time to time (even as in Hellas, centuries ago) the Coryphaeus tends it, shifting the fuel so that it burns brightlier. In Hellas, however enthralling a play might be, the actors never forgot that their first duty was one of reverence to him from whose worship drama was evolved; and here, at Bradfield, the old reverence is scrupulously reproduced, under the supervision of the Head-master. He sits there, the Headmaster, watching the play, clad in the scarlet robe worn by him in a Christian university; and among the audience, seated on the stone benches which rise in circular tiers around the arena, are many other clergy-men, most of them accompanied by wives, sisters, offspring, pupils. The white altar stands there in the midst, with its garland and its legend and its constant flame; yet not a word of protest is uttered, not a brow contracted. . . . Here, at least, I was to see a beautiful play, and to see it, as I soon found, under beautiful conditions. The way to the theatre lay down a long, steep dingle, through whose leaves the sunlight could not penetrate. When I came to the end of it, I seemed to emerge into the sunlight of ancient history. That altar, that flagged orchestra, those rough-hewn tiers of benches rising from the hollow; and above them, all around, the green trees, and wild flowers in full bloom! A trumpet was blown. A herald came upon the stage and thrice hailed us — citizens! The minstrels, attired in many colours, trooped across to their appointed places, holding their strange lyres and flutes. . . . And so the afternoon wore on, while we listened to the words of Aeschylus, in such sunlight and to such an accompaniment of birds as they had in Hellas, in such a theatre as that for which the poet wrote them.

Rare though performances of Greek drama may be, the plays live on in different guises. As the old myths inspired the Athenian dramatists, so their plays inspired those of later ages. The favourite classical themes provided basic material which subsequent ages could remodel in the light of their own experience and culture. Greek tragedy was rewritten in Latin by Nero's minister, Seneca. His plays, mostly modelled on Euripides, are markedly inferior to their originals, and may never have been intended for performance. Yet when the Renaissance revived interest in classical learning Seneca was studied and imitated ; his work had great influence on the drama of the period, and the revenge tragedy of the Elizabethans preserves, because of Seneca, the memory of Orestes returning to murder Clytemnestra.

So with comedy. Later Greek comic forms, developed by the Romans, were passed on to strolling Italian troupes, the Commedia dell' Arte, who worked with a stock company of comic types little different from those of Plautus — Pantaleone the foolish old man, the Dottore with his parade of knowledge ; the thwarted lovers Arlecchino and Colombina and comic servants like Pulcinello, one of the ancestors of our English Punch. Their improvised scripts influenced Goldoni in Italy and Molière in France ; in England they affected Shakespeare. Some comic types have endured through the centuries with little change. It is possible to trace a direct line from the fire-eating generals burlesqued by Aristophanes through the *miles gloriosus* of Roman comedy, Shakespeare's Pistol and Falstaff, and the 'bullies' of the Restoration theatre.

Nor have later dramatists been afraid of direct imitation. The greatest and most popular tragic theme of all is that of Oedipus. Besides the surviving masterpiece of Sophocles, it was treated by Aeschylus and Euripides and eight or nine other classical Greek writers. The Romans imitated their predecessors. Julius Caesar wrote tragedies for his own amusement, one of which was an *Oedipus*. In this he only followed the fashion, for among the Roman *élite* tragedy-writing enjoyed the same vogue as satirical verse in the Restoration. Seneca also wrote an *Oedipus*, and Nero, who fancied himself as an actor, took particular delight in playing the part.

When the seventeenth century took dramatists back to classical themes for inspiration, Corneille in 1657 and Dryden in 1679 wrote tragedies on the subject, as did Voltaire some years later. Nor has the story been confined to spoken drama. Stravinsky's *Oedipus Rex* sets it in dramatic oratorio form with a Latin libretto by Cocteau. Against a huge choir the leading characters are heard as soloists, with a linking commentary spoken by an impersonal Narrator. The meeting of Oedipus with the Sphinx was the subject of a ballet at Covent Garden in 1949. So Oedipus, with Faust and Don Juan, makes one of that select band of tragic heroes who appear on the stages of every country and every century, and whose stories can stand constant reinterpretation, for they are universal.

What are the Greek influences on the theatre of our own century? We have already mentioned Eliot's *Murder in the Cathedral*, which clothes a Christian subject in the forms of Greek tragedy. His *The Family Reunion* takes both form and subject-matter from the Greeks. It is based on the Orestes story: the hero, Harry, is a murderer returning to his home pursued by the avenging Furies, envisaged in their traditional Greek form. Harry's relatives form a chorus. *The Cocktail Party* is based on Euripides' *Alcestis*, though here the relationship is harder to perceive. Heracles, who interferes between life and death in the Greek play, is here replaced by a psychiatrist. *The Confidential Clerk* is a comedy of mistaken identity. Various interested parties lay claim to the hero ; whose son is he ? We are not far from the situations beloved of later Greek and Roman comedy.

Other countries have produced their own experiments. The work of the American Eugene O'Neill shows a preoccupation not only with the concepts but with the outward forms of the Greek theatre. He reverts to the use of masks to underline the symbolic meanings of his plays — *Lazarus Laughed* requires a chorus wearing forty-nine different kinds of masks — and makes frequent use of the Greek tragic ideal, individual man struggling against Fate. In *Anna Christie*, Fate is the sea, blamed for the troubles of the characters. Fate similarly dominates the story of *The Emperor Jones* in which the Negro ruler of a West Indian island is driven to death by his own fears. *Mourning becomes Electra* is a direct imitation of the Aeschylean trilogy, showing the workings of a family curse, even to the length of reduplicating the names of Aeschylus' characters.

In the modern French drama Greece has come into its own. The fashionable philosophy of Existentialism which influences many French writers insists on the futility of human existence. Happiness is illusion ; there are no ideals, no ultimate purpose. These playwrights found the Greek conception of an oppressive Fate thwarting individual intentions a perfect medium for their thoughts. Greek myths, and particularly Greek plays, have been rewritten with an existentialist slant. But where the Greeks were restrained and dignified the French dramatists are preoccupied with the sordid. The morbid and disgusting elements of the story are over-emphasized. Sophocles' *Antigone* shows the conflict between superhuman and human. After the disgrace of King Oedipus, Thebes was left under the rule of his sons Eteocles and Polyneices. They agreed to reign in alternate years, Eteocles first. At the end of his term of office he refused to withdraw. War followed, and the brothers died in single combat. The city is now ruled by their uncle Creon. He decrees that Eteocles shall be buried, but Polyneices, as an enemy of the state, must forgo the last rites. His sister, Antigone, determines to bury him herself. Her tragedy is that she thinks larger than the other characters in the play ; she sees what is right and must be done, while her opponents are bogged down in their narrow prejudices. Though Antigone finally dies, the victory is hers.

Anouilh's *Antigone* is on a lower plane. Antigone's defiance of Creon is dictated not so much by concern for her brother's soul as by lack of concern for her own. Even when it is revealed that in the carnage her brothers' bodies are unidentifiable, so that it is a matter of luck which is buried and which left to rot, she is still determined to die though her reasons are pointless. Anouilh uses the outward forms of Sophocles' play — a limited number of characters with the traditional Messenger, and a suave chorus in the person of one speaker — to express a far inferior message.

Similarly Sartre's *The Flies*, a treatment of the Orestes story, takes its title from the flies which are causing a plague in Argos ; they hang in clouds round the image of the vengeful god, who must be appeased in blood. The flies are forms of the Furies, and pursue Orestes after the murder. In some plays there is still a saving vein of poetry. Obey's rewriting of *Iphigeneia at Aulis*, the story of Agamemnon's sacrifice of his daughter, contains much that is beautiful in spite of a preoccupation with the death-wish. An interpolated character, the first Greek soldier to be killed on Trojan soil, expresses the futility of war. Unable to realize that he is dead, he hangs round his commander's tent trying to report, and attempts in vain to warn Iphigeneia when she is being lured to her death.

Cocteau's version of the Oedipus story, *The Infernal Machine*, is one of the best-known products of this school. Cocteau holds that the stories of the great heroes of the past belong to no particular time or place, and can just as well be transposed to our own day. This transposition is sometimes done by a complete change of setting, as in his film *Orphée*, which tells the Orpheus and Eurydice story in terms of modern France. Orpheus becomes an absinthe-sipping national poet, and Death is represented as an enigmatical princess in a black car with motor-cycle escort. Alternatively, the classical setting can be retained and modern concepts superimposed on it. In *The Infernal Machine* this is carried through to its extreme, so much so that the play is usually given in modern dress.

The immediate action of Sophocles' play — Oedipus' discovery that he has murdered his father Laius and married his own mother, and his consequent self-blinding — is compressed by Cocteau into a short last act. The events leading up to this — Oedipus' abandonment and adoption by the King of Corinth, his return to Thebes and conquest of the Sphinx, which Sophocles conveys with consummate skill as the main action is progressing — are extended and fully set out in the three long acts which precede. In

Act One the ghost of Laius appears on the ramparts of Thebes. Jocasta and Teiresias the High Priest visit the spot to make inquiries, but the ghost, though visible to the soldiers, is invisible to them. Act Two shows Oedipus' conquest of the Sphinx. Act Three is the wedding night of Oedipus and Jocasta. Memories and dreams of the past contrast with present problems and animosities. A linking chorus is provided by a disembodied voice constantly emphasizing the inability of the characters to escape their doom.

The first three acts are a prologue to the consummation of the tragedy in the fourth, but with a prologue three times as long as the tragedy the dramatic effect is immeasurably weakened. Sophocles achieves his effect by compression. Cocteau loses his by expansion. Sophocles is a master of dramatic irony ; statements harmless enough to the characters uttering them have a horrible significance for the audience, who know the full story. Cocteau strives for the same effect by imposing external images on the plot. In Act One Jocasta has constant trouble with her long scarf. Teiresias accidently treads on it, it tightens round her neck and she cries out. It is this scarf with which she hangs herself in Act Four. But such tricks are heavy-handed and their repetition irritating.

Cocteau sees Oedipus caught like a rat in a trap ; this shifts the audience's view-point. Sophocles placed the spectator on a level with the unhappy protagonist. He observed the events of the drama as if he were participating in them, sympathizing with Oedipus as one man with another. Cocteau sets him on a level with the gods. From this exalted position he watches in a spirit of rational detachment. Any human interest is ruled out. Thus

Oedipus' stature is inevitably diminished. When the Sophoclean hero blinds himself he rises to a new grandeur. Cocteau's Oedipus only sinks to a lower depth of degradation.

While this sort of writing is theatrically effective, its lasting value is dubious. Can we really use ancient drama-forms to present modern philosophies? Is it not rather a case of pouring new wine into old bottles? Stravinsky has said that 'the way to recreate classic dramas is to cool them, to bring them closer by making them more distant'. This opinion was shared by the French actor and director Louis Jouvet: 'To be fully understood a play must be restored to its own period, conventions, style . . . this invites us to put drama-forms back into their historical context, and create a sort of theatrical science, designed to illuminate the laws governing its structure'. Yet the extent to which the Greek drama can dominate the creations of an age over two thousand years distant shows that it is far from dead. Wherever there has been a stage, its plays have been copied, adapted and rewritten, and the Greek genius reveals itself in the superiority of the originals to their copies. As long as there is a serious theatre, dramatists will turn to Aeschylus and his successors for inspiration.

SOME NOTES ON PRODUCTION

O F all plays the Greek lose most by being deprived of their original setting. When all is said and done, Shakespeare does not suffer unduly in being transferred from the open to the proscenium stage. Attempts at reproducing Elizabethan conditions often seem fussy and irrelevant — it is the spirit of the play that matters, not the historical authenticity. A recent University Theatre project for Oxford envisaged a hall which could be adapted to form replicas of theatres of different periods — the Elizabethan apron, the Georgian theatre with its stage boxes and so forth — but this is to transform the drama from a living force into a series of museum pieces. But with Greek plays the problem is different. We are dealing with two distinct groups, actors and chorus, with widely different functions. To squash them all behind a proscenium makes this distinction meaningless. The chorus stand apart from the actors in spirit and should do so in practice also. On a stage the chorus is deprived of its essential freedom of movement, for few proscenium stages are large enough to take a full choral dance. Too often they spend half their time grouped in corners or squeezed into the wings so as not to interfere with the action, and the other half ranged in two rows like a team photograph declaiming perilously near the footlights. Greek plays demand space, and this means staging in the round. Perform in the open air if you can and dare ; if not, try putting actors and chorus in the centre of your hall and sitting spectators on the stage.

The first essential is a well-trained chorus. To do as some modern producers do and split the odes up between individual speakers is a mistake. The chorus should always speak in unison (except on those rare occasions, like the debate in *Agamemnon*, where individual lines are indicated in the text) or in parts. With the increased interest now being shown in choral speaking as elocution training this should not be difficult. Choose your chorus, even if it does not sing, as carefully as a choir, and balance the voices. Include a fair proportion of basses. Choruses composed entirely of women lack force and carrying power. Nor should the chorus be static. We do not know how Greek choruses danced ('Greek dancing' as now taught is Greek only in name), but some sort of unison movement should be attempted, as an accompaniment to the actors as well as when the audience is speaking. A recent production of *Lysistrata* made skilful use of modern Greek dance movements ; there is scope for the folk-dance expert here.

Actors, conversely, should not move too much. Speeches were declaimed, not spoken realistically, and gestures should be full and rhetorical rather than naturalistic. Be like the Peers in *Iolanthe*, 'dignified and stately'. Masks are a vexed question. It would be good to see them. Audiences unused to masked actors have no idea how effective they can be — the utter rigidity, for example, of a masked Creon rejecting Medea's impassioned plea is quite formidable. But modern actors, particularly amateurs, are not happy in masks without long practice, and audibility tends to suffer. Some producers use half-masks which leave the mouth free, but this is neither one thing nor the other. It is better to use either the full mask or a very heavy, stylized make-up. Hair on the masks seems to have been predominantly yellow. In some cases a very pale make-up is indicated — the god Dionysus, for example, in the *Bacchantes*.

Make the costumes colourful. We tend, for some reason,

to imagine the ancient world in monochrome, but nothing could be further from the truth. Remember that the Greeks painted their statues. It is certain that stage costumes were richly ornamented and highly coloured. Kings wore purple, some heroines yellow. Rhesus appeared in Euripides' play in golden armour. Black was then, as now, the colour of mourning. (Death in *Alcestis* has black wings.) Ghosts were probably dressed as corpses, with winding sheet and wreath. Kings carried sceptres, warriors spears and swords, heralds wreaths as symbols of their calling. Old men had staves. Detailed information about colour is not available, though vase-paintings give plentiful evidence for costume design. Above all, do not, as is so often done, send on the whole cast in white. Nothing is more deadly.

Settings need only be of the simplest. Often an existing architectural background can be called into use, a garden wall or entrance porch. If not, a simple background with three entrances is the most that will ever be required. Ornament it, if you wish, with columns and statues ; realistic painted scenery is not only unnecessary but entirely out of keeping with the spirit of the play. However good it may be, it will fight the actors, not help them. A square block will serve for an altar and, if necessary, a tomb. Different levels are useful ; actors and chorus at least should be on two levels if possible, and a flight of steps is invaluable in arranging interesting groupings. There is no need to go so far as Bradfield in reproducing every detail of the ancient performances, but by keeping the elements of the Greek setting your production will be assisted immeasurably.

Modern lighting techniques can be used to advantage without being incongruous. It is possible that some tragedians wrote the natural lighting effects into their plays — the first play to be performed in the day, for example, might mention the sunrise. Thus there is nothing wrong in reproducing these effects artificially. Lighting can also compensate for any lack of space by picking out actors from chorus ; dim lighting covers a multitude of sins.

For music, try modern Greek folk-tunes, or if these are not available, look nearer home. The author has successfully used Welsh folk-music for a production of the *Cyclops*. The choruses were adapted to some tunes, and others used as background for the rest of the play. Wales and Greece have much in common. The spirit of Welsh music is precisely right for Greek plays and collections of tunes are easily available. Keep the instrumentation simple. There is no need for full orchestral effects. The *Cyclops* production used a combination of recorder, timpani, and harp, an approximation to the Greek instruments. Violins are to be avoided as too romantic in tone for the severity of Greek tragedy. The Greeks also used castanets and maraccas! Trumpets can be used effectively in some plays, though there are excellent recordings of trumpet-calls for stage use.

Pace in the production is all-important. A Greek tragedy should flow from beginning to end without pause. Think in terms of dramatic oratorio rather than of drama proper. The Greeks used dramatic pauses sparingly and only to secure a special effect, like a few bars' rest in a symphony. For the most part characters entered during speeches, not in pauses between them ; even long processional entrances were covered by dialogue. Intervals are unnecessary when there is no scene-changing to be done. They are fatal to dramatic continuity, and it is not asking too much of an audience to expect them to sit through one tragedy without a break. Colour, speed and movement — let these be your guiding principles.

INDEX